W9-BOO-387

Kids Can Cook

REVISED EDITION

Vegetarian Recipes

by Dorothy R. Bates

How You Can Be Sure Your Child's Vegetarian Diet is Nutritious
Foreword by Suzanne Havala, MS, RD, FADA

Book Publishing Company

Summertown, Tenn.

Copyright 1987 Dorothy Bates
All rights reserved.

Printed in the United States
Book Publishing Company
PO Box 99
Summertown, TN 38483
1-888-260-8458 • www.bookpubco.com

Cover design: Estelle Carol
Interior design: Warren Jefferson
Interior photos: nancy Fleckenstein, Russ Honiker, Peter Schweitzer

ISBN 1-57067-086-2
ISBN13 978-1-57067-086-2

22 21 20   10 11 12 13

Cooks in the photgraphs:
Gretchen Bates
Erica Christopherson
Chris Cook
Sam Gaskin
Ben Rohrbach
Melina Sierra
Jody Stevenson
Vivian Traugot

Bates, Dorothy, R.
            Kids can cook: recipes kitchen-tested by kids for kid/by
        Dorothy R. Bates. --- Rev.ed
                        p.   c..
            Includes index.
            Summary: A collection of vegetarian and vegan recipes for breads, soups, main dishes, salads,
desserts, and party foods.
            ISBN 1-57067-086-2
            1. Vegetarian cookery Juvenile literature. [1. Vegetarian
        cookery 2. Cookery.] I Title
        641.5'636--dc21   99-35930
                                                 CIP

We chose to print this title on responsibly harvested paper stock certified by the Forest Stewardship Council,®
an independent auditor of responsible forestry practices. For more information, visit us.fsc.org.

FSC
www.fsc.org
MIX
Paper from
responsible sources
FSC® C005010

TABLE OF CONTENTS

How You Can Be Sure Your Child's Vegetarian Diet is Nutritious

Dorothy Bates couldn't have chosen a better time to write a vegetarian cookbook for kids and teens. A 1995 Roper Poll conducted for the Vegetarian Resource Group found that children between the ages of 8 and 12 years are becoming vegetarians at twice the rate of adults. They're doing it out of compassion for animals and a sincere concern for the environmental well-being of their planet. Many of these kids are going it alone, the only vegetarians in their households. You've got to admire that kind of courage and conviction.

But when Mom and Dad aren't vegetarians themselves, there can be some hand wringing over questions and concerns about the nutritional adequacy of a vegetarian diet for kids. Even in homes where vegetarianism is the norm, some people have lingering questions about vegetarian nutrition for kids. It's understandable, considering that vegetarian diets are outside our cultural norm. Most health care providers, school teachers, friends, and relatives don't have personal experience with a vegetarian lifestyle.

The fact is, a vegetarian diet is an excellent choice for any child. Vegetarian diets are associated with a decreased risk of coronary artery disease, some forms of cancer, high blood pressure, obesity, and diabetes. Children with an interest in going vegetarian need encouragement and support. However, feeding any child, vegetarian or not, takes time, patience, and care. That's where *Kids Can Cook* comes in.

A diet that is haphazard—heavy on chips, soft drinks, and fast food, and light on fruits and vegetables—is not likely to meet the needs of a growing child. On the other hand, a well-planned vegetarian diet offers kids health advantages over a nonvegetarian diet. With any luck, it will become a pattern for a lifetime. By helping your child to learn how to independently prepare nutritious, satisfying meals, you are giving your child the gift of a life skill that will serve him or her well for all the years to come. The recipes in *Kids Can Cook* will help you and your child get started.

A Word About Nutrition

Vegetarian and vegan diets that contain adequate calories and a variety of foods can meet all of the nutritional needs of kids and teens and are associated with health advantages. Even so, when it comes to designing a vegetarian diet for kids and teens, a few key nutrients deserve special attention.

Protein: The best way to ensure that your child gets enough protein is to make sure she gets enough calories to meet her energy needs as well as a reasonable variety of foods, including fruits, vegetables, grains, legumes, nuts, and seeds. When a child's diet is too low in calories, the

body will burn protein for energy. When there are enough calories in the diet, protein can be used for building new tissues instead.

Some vegetarian foods that are especially good sources of protein and are popular with children are:

- Bean burritos and tacos
- Veggie burgers
- Veggie hotdogs
- Hummus or other bean dip with vegetable sticks or tortilla chips
- Peanut butter on apple chunks or celery sticks
- Peanut butter sandwiches or crackers
- Tofu salad sandwiches
- Soymilk and fruit smoothies
- Tofu or nonfat ricotta cheese and vegetable lasagne
- Vegetarian pizza
- Nonfat or soy yogurt
- Nonfat or soy cheese on crackers
- Tempeh sloppy Joes

Calcium: Children and teens are in a period of rapid and growth and development, and they need plenty of calcium in their diets to accommodate the growth and development of their teeth and bones. There are several factors, including the presence of vitamin D, the amounts of animal protein and sodium in the diet, and others that affect the body's ability to absorb and retain calcium. These factors are equally as important as having adequate amounts of calcium in the diet. Nevertheless, it's a good idea to encourage three servings of calcium-rich foods each day. Aim for big servings—a cup at a time.

What? Your kids won't eat vegetables? More about that challenge in a moment. Keep in mind, however, that calcium-fortified orange juice and fortified soymilk are easy ways to add calcium to the hit-or-miss diet of older kids and teens.

Iron: Many of the foods that are high in calcium also happen to be high in iron. Some examples include dried beans and peas, dark, green, leafy vegetables, and dried fruits. There are many others. Serving foods that are high in vitamin C with meals also increases the body's absorption of the iron. Examples of foods that are rich sources of vitamin C include broccoli, cabbage, oranges, tomatoes, green peppers, potatoes, and many others.

Vitamin B12: If your child is a vegan and eats no animal products at all, then he needs a regular and reliable source of vitamin B12 such as vitamin B12-fortified foods (fortified soymilk, breakfast cereals, and others) or a vitamin B12 supplement. If there's any doubt about whether fortified foods are providing enough vitamin B12, the safest bet is to have your kids take a supplement.

Vitamin D: The important thing to remember about vitamin D and children is that vitamin D, together with calcium, is critical for the normal growth and development of bones and teeth. If you have any doubts about whether or not your child is at risk of not getting enough vitamin D, ask a registered dietitian or your health care provider for an assessment and recommendation.

Summing It Up
The science of nutrition can get a bit complicated, but eating well is a relatively simple matter. The most important points to remember are:
- Adequate calories
- A reasonable variety of foods
- A reliable source of vitamin B12 for vegan and near-vegan children and adequate vitamin D
- Limits on junk foods that displace more nutritious foods from the diet

Make Fruits and Vegetables Your Child's Best Friends:
If it seems as though fruits and vegetables can't win over chips and candy bars, take heart. You already know that you're facing a losing battle when you try to force people to do things they don't want to do. Kids are no exception. However, there are some strategies that will dramatically elevate the popularity of healthful foods in your child's eye.

- *Set the Example:* Model the behavior that you want your children to adopt. If you want your child to like broccoli and sweet potatoes, let them see you enjoying them yourself. However, don't pretend to like something you don't. Kids can spot a fake. If you don't care for a food, fix it for the others in your household, and don't make a big show out of the fact that there isn't any on your plate.

- *Attitude is Everything:* Present foods with a positive attitude. It will make all the difference in the world. At the same time, don't push. Present food with an air that says that you have every reason to expect that your family is going to like it.

- *No Need to Be the Hall Monitor:* Don't try to be the diet police. You don't have to eat foods that you don't like; let your child express food preferences too. We don't all like the same foods. If your child expresses a dislike for a food, play it low-key. She may come around in time. If not, that's okay too. There are hundreds of vegetables, fruits, and grains. If your child doesn't like one or another, there are plenty of others to take its place.

- *Permit Freedom of Choice:* Children prefer a measure of freedom like everyone else. If your child turns up his nose at a particular food, offer one or two other choices. If your child still refuses, let it go. The next meal will bring new choices.

- *The Family That Plans Meals Together Eats Together:* Get your children involved in meal planning. Ask for their ideas and preferences. Then take your children shopping for food. Children are more likely to eat what they've had a hand in choosing. If you are buying tomatoes, let your child pick out two or three and put them into the bag. Give older children even more responsibility. Send your teen to the opposite side of the produce aisle to pick out a cantaloupe. Who cares if it's the best one? It's more important that your kids become involved.

- *Promote the Spirit of Adventure:* Have some fun experimenting with new fruits and vegetables. Try something challenging, like a really strange-looking piece of exotic fruit. If you get it home and find that you don't like it, that's okay. It's part of the process of trying new things. Sometimes you find a new favorite, and sometimes you encounter a dud.

- *Fix Meals Together:* Your kids are more likely to eat foods they've had a hand in fixing. Supervise young children and let them help with simple tasks like retrieving foods from the pantry or dumping prepared ingredients into a pot. Older kids can help wash and peel fruits and vegetables for salads and assemble ingredients for soups and casseroles.

- *Grow Your Own Food:* Show your kids how food grows and help them develop an interest and appreciation for fresh foods. Plant a window sill herb garden, grow a pot of tomatoes on your back porch or apartment balcony, or plant a full-sized backyard garden—whatever makes sense for your lifestyle, small scale or large.

Teach your children to care about their food. Encourage them to be comfortable, independent, and creative in the kitchen. Show them that *Kids Can Cook* and your legacy will be a healthful eating style that will protect and support them all of their lives.

Suzanne Havala, MS, RD, FADA
Nutrition Advisor, The Vegetarian Resource Group and
author of *The Complete Idiot's Guide to Being Vegetarian*

A Meal Planning Guide for Children

The meal planning guide that follows is suitable for school-aged children up to 12 years of age. The guide excludes all animal products. If you prefer to include dairy products and/or eggs, they can be substituted for soy products where indicated. For more information about planning nutritious vegetarian meals for kids and teens, contact the *Vegetarian Resource Group* (address and web site below).

Meal Planning Guide for Children

Food Group	Number of Servings
Grains	6 or more for 4 to 6 year olds; 7 or more for 7 to 12 year olds (A serving is 1 slice of bread or $^1/_2$ cup cooked cereal or grain or pasta or $^1/_2$ cup to 1 cup ready-to-eat cereal.)
Legumes, Nuts, Seeds	$1^1/_2$ to 3 for 4 to 6 year olds; 3 or more for 7 to 12 year olds (A serving is $^1/_2$ cup cooked beans, tofu, tempeh or textured soy; or 3 ounces of meat analog; or 2 Tbsp nuts, seeds, nut or seed butter.)
Fortified Soymilk	3 (A serving is 1 cup fortified soymilk.)
Vegetables	1 to $1^1/_2$ for 4 to 6 year olds; 4 or more for 7 to 12 year olds (A serving is $^1/_2$ cup cooked or 1 cup raw vegetables.)
Fruits	2 for 4 to 6 year olds; 3 or more for 7 to 12 year olds (A serving is $^1/_2$ cup canned fruit or $^1/_2$ cup juice, or 1 medium fruit.)
Fats	4 for 4 to 6 year olds; 5 for 7 to 12 year olds (A serving is 1 teaspoon margarine or oil.)

Adapted from *Simply Vegan*, Third Edition, by Reed Mangels, PhD, RD and Debra Wasserman. Reprinted with permission from The Vegetarian Resource Group, PO Box 1463, Baltimore, Maryland, 21203; www.vrg.org; 410-366-8343.

Introduction

Kids like to cook if given a chance. For more than ten years, teenagers from the Farm School, a private school located at The Farm in Summertown, Tenn., have come to my house on Friday afternoons to prepare a three-course dinner. They set a pretty table, and we all sit down to enjoy the meal. They found that all it takes to cook successfully is to follow directions step by step.

As their skill levels increased, they found trying new recipes an adventure, and their requests and suggestions ("Can we make my grandma's kolacky?") have enriched my own recipe collection. A summer program

at The Farm, "Kids to the Country," gives me the opportunity to cook with disadvantaged inner-city children.

The genuine joy these kids had in cooking and the enthusiasm they brought inspired this book. I appreciate the many happy hours we spend together and dedicate this book to kids everywhere who like to cook and eat.

Dorothy R. Bates

Secrets of Successful Cooks

Cooking is like riding a bicycle—the more you do it, the better you get. Just remember:

1. Always read the recipe all the way through first.
2. Get out all the ingredients—these are in bold face. As soon as you have used the baking powder, baking soda, salt, or spices, put that container away so you don't use it twice.
3. Set out the tools and pans you will need. After you use one, put it in the sink to keep your work area neat.
4. Wash your hands before you start. An apron will protect your clothes from stains. Tie back long hair so it doesn't get in your way (and in the food!)
5. Wash tools and clean your countertop as you go along to make final clean-up easy.
6. Ask for help with heavy or hot pans or pots. If you are not sure how to do something, ask someone.

For your safety:

1. Turn pan handles toward the back of the stove so the pan can't be bumped off.
2. Always use pot holders or oven mitts to lift lids off pans or remove food from the oven. Check the position of oven racks before you turn on the oven.
3. Handle knives, peelers, and graters carefully—watch your fingers!
4. Treat machines with respect. Ask someone to show you how to work them. Don't put your hand into a food processor or blender—those blades are sharp!

Useful Tools

Bread Knife

Colander

Masher

Spatula

Measuring Cups
& Spoons

Rolling Pin

Wooden Board

Grater

Paring Knife

Rubber
Scraper

Slotted
Spoon

Brush

Wooden
Spoons

Peeler

Juicer

Pastry Blender

Timer

Whisks

Ingredients

Ingredients are listed in bold face type in the recipes. Make sure you read the whole recipe and have everything you need before you start.

When measuring: Use level measurement, scooping up a dry ingredient to overflow the spoon, then leveling it off with the back of a knife. When measuring honey or other sticky ingredients, it helps to grease the cup or spoon first. To measure brown sugar, pack it into a measuring cup. Use a clean cup for dry ingredients.

Egg replacer: Ener-G Egg Replacer is an easy-to-use substitute for eggs. Because it is a powder, you can keep it on your kitchen shelf until you're ready to use it. Look for it at your local natural foods store.

Flour: We used unbleached all-purpose flour. Some people prefer whole wheat flour or pastry flour. You can substitute what you have and experiment.

Nutritional Yeast: Use only good tasting nutritional yeast (saccharomyces cerevisiae). Red Star Vegetarian Support Formula® is a good choice. It comes in yellow flakes, has a cheesy flavor, and supplies protein and B-vitamins.

Softened butter or margarine: Soften by slicing thinly onto a plate, or hold wrapped stick in your hands.

Sweeteners: If you prefer to use an alternative to sugar, try FruitSource or Sucanat; you can also substitute brown rice syrup or liquid fructose for honey. Look for these in your local natural foods store.

Tempeh: A soybean cake bound together by delicious mushroom fibers. Found in the freezer section of natural foods stores. Great steamed and deep-fried.

Tofu: Some brands are softer, some are firmer. It can be frozen in the package and darkens in color. Thaw frozen tofu before using, and squeeze out excess liquid.

Texturized Soy Protein, Tempeh and Miso: These are all soybean products available in health food stores. All are good sources of protein, vitamins, and minerals, and are low in calories and cholesterol-free.

Breakfast & Quick Breads

Breads of all kinds are fun to make, and it's not difficult to make hot breads. These rise because of the baking powder or soda in the recipe and go with any meal.

☀ indicates easy-to-make recipe

☀Pancakes

Makes 10 to 12 pancakes

You can tell the griddle is ready if a few drops of water sprinkled on it bounce. Some griddles need oil. Always make a test pancake first to see if the pan is hot enough.

1. Heat a heavy griddle on *medium* high.

2. Measure into a medium bowl:

     2 cups flour
     1 tablespoon baking powder
     1 tablespoon honey or sugar
     2 tablespoons oil
     2 cups milk or soymilk

   Stir together. The batter will be lumpy.

3. Use a 1/3-cup measure to scoop out batter for the test cake. It will be ready to turn over when bubbles appear on top. If it browns too fast, lower the heat. Continue until all the batter is used up. Cover the pancakes with a clean dish towel to keep warm.

Chris sifts flour before measuring.

Waffles

Makes about 6 waffles

Read the directions for the waffle iron you use. Most have indicator lights that turn off when the iron is hot enough to begin cooking. Oil the iron if needed. The waffle is done when the iron stops steaming. Don't open the lid to peek while it is cooking!

1. Sift into a medium bowl:

    2 cups flour

    1 tablespoon baking powder

    1/2 teaspoon salt

2. In a small bowl, beat together with a whisk:

    2 eggs*   1/4 cup canola oil

    1 tablespoon honey or sugar   1 1/2 cups milk or soymilk

    1/2 to 1 cup chopped pecans (optional)

3. Stir the liquids into flour mixture, but don't overmix.

4. Use a cup to pour batter onto the heated waffle iron. Make a test waffle first; then you will know how much batter to use. Bake until no steam comes out. The waffle should be golden brown.

NOTE: For fluffier waffles, separate the eggs, mixing the yolks in with the liquids. Beat the whites to form soft peaks. Fold the beaten whites into the batter just before cooking.

*Vegan Alternative: Instead of 2 eggs, you can use 1 tablespoon Ener-G Egg replacer mixed with 1/4 cup water or 4 teaspoons flaxseed blended with 1/4 cup warm water in a blender until thickened.

☀French Toast

Makes 4 slices

*J*ust the thing for breakfast if you have some bread that's not fresh enough for sandwiches.

1. Stir in a shallow bowl to mix well:

   1 egg or 3 tablespoons nutritional yeast flakes

   1/2 cup milk

   1/2 teaspoon sugar

2. Have ready to dip into the mixture:

   4 slices "day-old" bread

3. Heat in a frying pan over medium-high:

   1 tablespoon oil

4. Dip each slice of bread into the egg mix, coating both sides. Fry in the hot oil until golden brown. Do one or two slices at a time. Add a little oil to the pan if needed to keep the toast from sticking.

☀Honey Topping

Makes about 1/4 cup

1. Cream together until fluffy:

   1/2 stick butter or margarine

   2 tablespoons honey

2. Put a spoonful on top of each waffle or piece of French Toast.

Baking Powder Biscuits

Makes about 15 biscuits

Biscuits are not only good for breakfast. You can make these for lunch or dinner too, to go with fresh corn on the cob in summer and a hot soup in the winter.

1. Heat the oven to 425°. Lightly oil a baking sheet.

2. Sift together into a medium bowl:

   2 cups flour
   1 tablespoon baking powder
   $1/2$ teaspoon salt

3. Measure out and stir into the flour mix:

   $1/3$ cup canola oil
   $1/2$ cup milk

4. Lightly flour a rolling pin and board.

5. With some flour on your hands, pat the dough out and roll it to about $1/2$-inch thick, using a light rolling stroke. Cut out biscuits using a 2-inch cookie cutter or an empty tin can. Don't twist the cutter; just press down and lift the biscuits onto the baking sheet with a spatula. Push the scraps together into a ball, and lightly roll out for more biscuits.

6. Put in the hot oven, and set the timer for 12 minutes. Peek at them and if not lightly browned on top, bake a few minutes more. Remove from the baking sheet, and serve warm.

☀Drop Biscuits

Makes about 18 biscuits

These can be made quickly, while the oven heats.

1. Follow the directions for Baking Powder Biscuits on page 13, but increase the milk to 1 cup. The dough should be soft enough to push off by the spoonful onto the lightly oiled baking sheet. Set the timer for 12 minutes, and bake in the hot oven.

☀Drop Cheese Biscuits

Makes about 18 biscuits

1. Follow directions to make Drop Biscuit dough. After you add the milk for the soft dough, stir in one of these:

> **1 cup grated jack cheese or**
>
> **1 cup grated soy jack cheese or**
>
> **1/4 cup nutritional yeast**

2. If the dough is too stiff to drop, add a little more milk. It should be soft. Drop by the spoonful onto the oiled baking sheet. Set the timer for 10 to 12 minutes, and bake in the hot oven.

Erica puts Drop Cheese Biscuits on a baking sheet.

Irish Soda Bread

Makes 10 slices

Celebrate St. Patrick's Day in March with this traditional loaf.

1. Preheat the oven to 350°. Lightly oil a small baking sheet, or spray with nonstick cooking spray.

2. Mix in a large bowl:
    1 1/2 cups whole wheat pastry flour
    1 1/2 cups unbleached white flour
    1/4 cup sugar
    1 teaspoon baking soda
    1 teaspoon salt

3. Stir in:
    1/2 cup currants or raisins
    1/4 cup oil
    1 cup sour milk or soymilk*

4. Knead the mixture in the bowl 5 times, turn out on a lightly floured surface, and put flour on your hands to lightly knead 10 times.

5. Shape the dough into a round loaf, and place on the baking sheet. Use a floured, serrated knife to make a 4-inch long, 1-inch deep X across the top.

6. Set the timer for 45 to 50 minutes, and bake until the bread is golden brown and sounds hollow if you tap the top. Cool.

* To make sour milk, add 1 teaspoon vinegar to 1 cup plain milk, and let it stand a little.

Muffins

Makes 12 muffins

The secret of light muffins is not overmixing the batter; try to combine the wet and dry ingredients with as few strokes as possible. The batter will be lumpy.

1. Coat 12 large muffin tins with oil, or use baking cup liners in the tins. Heat the oven to 350°.

2. Sift together into a medium bowl:

    2 cups flour   1/4 cup sugar

    2 teaspoons baking powder 1/2 teaspoon salt

3. With a large spoon, make a well in the center of the dry ingredients.

4. In a small bowl, whisk together:

    1 egg* 1/2 cup oil

    3/4 cup water

5. Pour the wet ingredients into the well, and combine the wet and dry ingredients, stirring only 20 to 25 times with a large spoon. It's okay for the batter to be lumpy.

6. Spoon the mixture into the oiled muffin tins, filling each about 2/3 full.

7. Set the timer for 20 to 25 minutes, and bake in the hot oven until lightly browned on top.

8. Run a knife around the edge of each muffin tin to loosen the muffins before lifting out to a serving plate.

Blueberry Muffins

Makes 12 muffins

Blackberries are very good in muffins too.

1. Pick over, rinse and dry on paper towels:

   1 cup fresh blueberries

2. Prepare the recipe for Muffins on page 17. Gently stir in the berries after mixing the wet and dry ingredients. Be careful not to overmix. Continue with the recipe.

Date Muffins

Makes 12 muffins

The natural sweetness of dates makes them a perfect addition to muffins.

1. Prepare the recipe on page 17 for Muffins, but before adding the liquids to the dry ingredients, put into the flour mixture:

   1/2 cup chopped, pitted dates

2. Stir the dates around in the flour to coat evenly. Then add the liquid ingredients, and continue with the muffin recipe.

*Vegan Alternative for all muffins: Instead of 1 egg, you can use 1/2 tablespoon Ener-G Egg replacer mixed with 2 tablespoons water or 2 teaspoons flaxseed blended with 2 tablespoons warm water in a blender until thickened.

☀Raisin Bran Muffins

Makes 12 muffins

Using raisin bran breakfast cereal to make these muffins may seem unusual, but you'll really like the results.

1. Heat the oven to 400°. Oil 12 muffin tins or use baking cup liners.

2. Mix together in a large bowl:

   2½ cups raisin bran cereal   1 cup milk or soymilk**

   ½ cup sugar 3 tablespoons oil

   1 egg*

   1 tablespoon grated orange rind (optional)

3. When these are mixed, sift into the bowl:

   1¼ cups flour   1 tablespoon baking powder

4. Combine the bran mix with the flour mix in as few strokes as possible. The batter will be lumpy.

5. Spoon the batter into the muffin tins. Set the timer for 20 minutes, and bake in the hot oven. If the muffins are not lightly browned on top after 20 minutes, bake a few minutes more. Remove from the tins while warm. (Run a knife around the edge of each muffin if needed to loosen it.)

*Vegan Alternative: Instead of 1 egg, you can use ½ tablespoon Ener-G Egg replacer mixed with 2 tablespoons water or 2 teaspoons ground flaxseed blended with 2 tablespoons warm water in a blender until thickened.

**You can use sour milk or yogurt if you wish. Use only 2 teaspoons baking powder and add ½ teaspoon baking soda.

Cornbread In A Skillet

Makes 8 servings

Baking this in a heated pan makes a crusty bottom. This can also be baked in a 9 x13-inch pan instead of a skillet.

1. Heat the oven to 375˚.

2. Put into a heavy 10-inch cast-iron skillet:
   2 tablespoons oil

3. Put the pan in the oven to heat. (Have potholders ready for lifting it out.)

4. While the oven and pan are heating, mix together in a medium-sized bowl:
   2 cups yellow cornmeal   2 cups flour
   1 teaspoon salt   5 teaspoons baking powder
   2 tablespoons sugar

5. Make a well in the center of the dry ingredients. Pour into the well:
   2 cups water, milk, or soymilk
   1/3 cup oil

6. Use a big spoon to stir the wet and dry ingredients together, mix them well.

7. Carefully lift the hot pan out of the oven, pour the cornbread batter into the pan, then set the pan back in the oven to bake.

8. Set the timer for 30 minutes, and bake in the hot oven. It should be lightly browned on top and pulling away from the edges of the pan.

Jalapeño Cornbread

Wear gloves to handle hot peppers.

1. Remove and discard the seeds from 2 or 3 jalapeño peppers. Mince the peppers very small, and add to the batter for Cornbread in a Skillet.

Corn Cakes

Makes 18 cakes

1. Measure into a medium bowl:

   2 cups flour

   $1/4$ cup sugar

   2 teaspoons baking powder

   $1/2$ teaspoon baking soda

   $1/2$ teaspoon salt

2. Stir the dry ingredients well, then add:

   $1/4$ cup canola oil

   $1^1/2$ cups milk

   1 cup whole kernel corn

3. Heat a heavy pan or griddle, spreading a teaspoon of oil over it with a pancake turner. When the pan is hot, drop large spoonfuls of corn batter onto the griddle. Cook on one side until bubbles appear; then turn over. Cook the other side until lightly browned. Serve hot.

Banana Nut Bread

Makes 1 loaf (16 slices)

Simple to make and simply delicious.

1. Oil a 9 x 5-inch loaf pan. Heat the oven to 350°.

2. In a medium bowl, cream together using a slotted spoon:
   $1/2$ cup oil
   1 cup sugar

3. Sift onto a piece of waxed paper:
   2 cups unbleached flour   **3 teaspoons baking powder**
   $1/2$ teaspoon salt

4. Add the flour mixture to the bowl, and stir until the batter is well mixed and quite smooth.

5. Stir into the batter:
   2 well-mashed bananas   **$1/2$ cup chopped walnuts**

6. Spoon the mixture into the oiled loaf pan. Set the timer for 45 minutes, and bake in the hot oven.

7. Test for doneness by sticking a toothpick into the center of the loaf. If it comes out clean, the bread is done. Remove the pan from the oven, and let it cool for 10 minutes. Then remove the loaf from the pan.

Note: For Cranberry Nut Bread, add 1 cup chopped, washed and drained cranberries instead of the bananas.

Date Nut Bread

Makes 1 loaf (18 slices)

This is delicious sliced thinly and spread with cream cheese, or made into little sandwiches for a party.

1. Oil a 9 x 5-inch loaf pan. Heat the oven to 325°.

2. Place in a 2-quart saucepan, and cook over medium heat, stirring, for 5 minutes:
   1¹/₂ cups dates, pitted and chopped
   ³/₄ cup hot water

3. Remove the pan from the heat, and stir in:
   ³/₄ cup chopped walnuts   ¹/₄ cup canola oil
   ¹/₂ cup sugar 1 teaspoon vanilla

4. Let this mixture cool. While it cools, sift together onto waxed paper:
   2 cups flour
   1 teaspoon baking soda

5. Stir the flour into the cooled date-nut mixture.

6. Spoon the batter into the oiled pan. Set the timer for 1 hour, and bake in the hot oven. (You may need to bake it 10 minutes or so more.) Stick a toothpick in the center of the loaf. When it comes out clean, bread is done.

7. Remove the loaf from the oven, and cool for 5 minutes, then turn out of the pan. Cool completely before slicing, and use a very sharp knife to slice thinly. Wrap the loaf well and store in the refrigerator.

Coffee Cake

Makes 9 servings

A very special breakfast treat you can make ahead.

1. Oil a 9 x 9-inch pan. Preheat the oven to 375°.

2. Mix with a slotted spoon in a medium bowl:
   1/2 cup oil
   1/2 cup sugar
   1/2 cup milk or soymilk

3. Sift in and stir together:
   2 cups flour
   2 teaspoons baking powder
   1/2 teaspoon salt

4. When the batter is well mixed, spread it in the pan.

5. Mix together in a small bowl:
   1/2 cup sugar
   1/2 cup flour
   1/2 teaspoon cinnamon
   1/2 stick margarine or butter, softened

6. Sprinkle this mixture evenly over the batter.

7. Set the timer for 45 minutes. Bake in the hot oven. Cut into squares to serve.

☀Peanut Butter Bread

Makes 1 loaf

If any bread is left over, it's very good toasted.

1. Oil a 9 x 5-inch loaf pan. Heat the oven to 350°.

2. Measure into a bowl and set aside:
    2 cups flour
    2 teaspoons baking powder

3. Stir well to mix:
    1/2 cup peanut butter
    1/4 cup honey or sugar

4. When it is well mixed, stir in the flour. Work it all together with a slotted spoon until no flour shows.

5. Stir in:
    1 cup milk or soymilk

6. Stir until the milk is well mixed in. Then spoon the batter into the oiled loaf pan.

7. Set the timer for 45 to 50 minutes, and bake in the hot oven. The loaf will be lightly browned on top and pulling away from the sides of the pan when it is done.

Granola

Makes 8 cups

The rolled oats you use to make granola is regular long-cooking oatmeal (not the instant kind).

1. Preheat the oven to 350°. Mix in a large bowl:

   4 cups rolled oats

   1 cup chopped raw almonds

   1 cup raw sunflower seeds

   2 cups raisin bran flakes

2. Heat together in a small pan:

   $1/2$ cup brown sugar

   $3/4$ cup canola oil

   $1/3$ cup water

   Add:

   2 tablespoons vanilla

3. Stir the liquids into the oat mixture, and mix well.

4. Pour out onto a cookie sheet with sides. Use a pancake turner to push the mix in from the edges of the pan on all sides, leaving an inch of pan bare. Set timer for 45 minutes, and bake in the hot oven. Every 10 minutes, remove the pan and mix the granola with the turner. Leave the edges of the pan bare to prevent burning. Put the pan back in the oven.

5. Cool the mix and store in an airtight jar or in plastic bags in the freezer.

Gretchen puts Cuban Bread, p. 32, in a basket for serving.

Yeast Breads

Nothing smells better than bread or rolls baking in the oven, and yeast doughs are fun to make.

You must be careful of the water temperature you use with yeast. Water that is too hot or too cold will kill the yeast or slow its action. Test the temperature with your fingers to be sure the water is lukewarm. Honey, molasses, or sugar added to the yeast will help it rise the bread. You'll find that flours vary in the amount of liquid they absorb. If the dough feels real sticky, add more flour. Be sure the oven is the correct temperature, and set the timer to the proper baking time.

☻ indicates easy-to-make recipe

☀Cuban Bread

Makes 2 loaves

This is an easy bread for beginners to make.

1. Into a large bowl, measure:
    1 tablespoon dry yeast
    1 tablespoon honey or sugar
    1 tablespoon canola oil
    2 cups warm water

2. Stir the yeast mixture until it is completely dissolved. Add one cup at a time:
    6 or 7 cups flour

    Flours vary in the amount of liquid they will absorb; add enough flour so the dough isn't sticky.

3. To knead, roll the dough around on a floured surface, then pat down and fold over, press, turn the dough, fold again, press down, and turn. Continue kneading for 5 to 10 minutes until the dough feels smooth and elastic. Oil a large bowl, put the dough in, and turn it around to coat the dough with oil. Cover the bowl with a towel, and let set in a warm place for 45 minutes, or until it is double in size.

4. Punch the dough down completely, then spread a little oil on top. Cover the bowl with a towel, and let it rise again until doubled in size. Punch down the dough and divide it in half.

5. Prepare a baking sheet by sprinkling it with cornmeal or by lightly oiling it.

6. Shape the dough into 2 long loaves, and place them on the baking sheet. Using a sharp knife, cut a few slashes in the top of each loaf. Set the timer and let the loaves rise 10 minutes.

7. Put a 9 x 13-inch baking pan filled with hot water on the bottom shelf of the oven. Set the loaves on the shelf above it. Close the oven door, turn the oven on to 400°, set the timer for 45 minutes, and bake the bread. This bread is best served warm.

☀Hot Garlic Bread

Makes 1 loaf

1. Heat the oven to 375°.

2. Cut in half lengthwise:
   1 loaf Cuban Bread

3. Mix together
   1 cup canola or olive oil
   3 sliced garlic cloves

4. Brush on the halves of the loaf. Cut the halves into 2-inch slices, and put on a cookie sheet.

5. Set the timer for 15 minutes, and bake in the hot oven.

☀Oatmeal Molasses Bread

Makes 2 loaves

The rolled oats you use to make this bread are the regular, long-cooking kind, not instant oatmeal.

1. Combine in a big bowl:

   1 cup rolled oats **2 cups hot water**

2. In a small bowl, combine until dissolved:

   1 tablespoon dry yeast **$1/3$ cup warm water**
   1 tablespoon molasses

3. Add to the oatmeal in the big bowl:

   2 tablespoons oil **$1/3$ cup molasses**

4. Stir this mixture with a wooden spoon, then add the yeast mix. Slowly stir in:

   5 to 6 cups flour **1 teaspoon salt**

5. When well mixed, cover the bowl and put in a warm place to rise until it is double in size.

6. Oil two loaf pans.

7. Press down the dough, divide in half, and put into the pans. Lay a towel over the tops of the pans, and let the bread rise again. When it is almost double in size, heat the oven to 325°.

8. Set the timer for 55 minutes, and bake the loaves in the hot oven.

9. Remove the pans from the oven to a bread board, and let cool for 10 minutes before you take the loaves out of the pans.

Monkey Pull Apart Bread

Makes

It's interesting to see what happens when balls of yeasted bread dough are baked close together, like in this "pull-apart" bread.

1. Combine in a medium bowl, and let set for 10 minutes:

    1 tablespoon dry yeast   **¹/₂ cup warm water**

2. Add and stir well

    ¹/₄ cup canola oil   **¹/₃ cup sugar**
    1 teaspoon salt   **2 cups white unbleached flour**
    1¹/₂ cups whole wheat pastry flour

3. Turn out the dough on a floured surface to knead until smooth. (See Step 3 in the recipe for Cuban Bread, p. 32 for instructions on how to knead bread.) Put in a large, oiled bowl, and turn the dough around to coat with the oil. Cover with a towel and let rise in a warm place for 1 hour, or until double in size. Oil a tube pan and set aside.

4. Mix together and set aside:

    ³/₄ cup brown sugar   **1 teaspoon cinnamon**
    ¹/₂ cup chopped walnuts

5. Pour a little oil in a saucer. Punch down the dough and shape into balls the size of a golf ball. Dip each ball in the oil, then roll in the sugar mix. Put into the tube pan in a single layer, barely touching. Place any additional balls on top.

6. Cover the pan and let rise 45 minutes. Heat the oven to 375°. Set the timer for 40 minutes, and bake the bread in the hot oven. Remove and place a plate over the top of the pan. Using potholders, carefully turn the pan upside down on the plate. The monkey bread should come out after a minute or so.

Basic Rolls

Makes 16 rolls

1. Stir together in a large bowl:
   - 1 tablespoon dry yeast
   - 1/4 cup warm water
   - 1 tablespoon honey or sugar

2. Let the yeast dissolve, then stir in:
   - 2 tablespoons oil
   - 1 cup warm water

3. Stir in:
   - 1 teaspoon salt
   - 3 1/2 to 4 cups flour

4. Knead well. If the dough is sticky, add a little more flour.

5. Pat a little oil on the dough, cover the bowl with a towel, and let it rise in a warm place until it is double in size. This takes about 1 hour.

6. Oil a baking sheet. With oil on your fingers, press down the dough and divide it into 4 smaller balls. From each ball, shape 4 round rolls, and put them on the baking sheet. With your fingertip, lightly oil the tops of the rolls. Let them rise for 10 minutes while the oven is heating.

7. Heat the oven to 400°. When the oven is hot, set the timer for 30 minutes, and bake the rolls until they are lightly browned on top.

☀Sesame Seed Rolls

Makes 16 rolls

1. Prepare **Basic Rolls** from the facing page up to step #6:
2. Place in a saucer:
   2 tablespoons sesame seeds
3. As you shape each roll, dip the top into the seeds. You can also use either:
   2 tablespoons caraway seeds, or
   2 tablespoons flax seeds
4. Continue with the recipe.

Breadsticks

Makes 20 breadsticks

Breadsticks are delicious with caraway or sesame seeds on top. Brush the sticks with oil before you sprinkle on the seeds, so the seeds will stay on while baking.

1. Prepare **Basic Rolls** from the facing page up to step #6:

2. Pinch off a small ball of dough, and roll it between your hands into sticks about 6 inches long and $\frac{1}{2}$-inch thick. Place the sticks on an oiled baking sheet.

3. Oil the tops of the sticks, and sprinkle with your choice of seeds. Let rise 10 minutes while the oven heats.

4. Set the timer for 10 minutes, and bake, then reduce the heat to 350°, set the timer for 10 minutes more, and bake at the lower temperature. Watch carefully so the sticks don't burn.

Basic Fancy Roll Dough

Makes 24 rolls

This is the kids' absolute favorite to make and shape.

1. In a large bowl, dissolve:
    1 tablespoon yeast
    $1/2$ cup warm water
    $1/3$ cup sugar

2. Stir this and add:
    $1/2$ cup oil
    1 cup flour

3. Mix this well, then add:
    $3/4$ cup water

4. Stir well, then stir in 1 cup at a time:
    $3^1/_2$ to 4 cups unbleached white flour

    Dough should be soft but not sticky. Turn out onto a floured surface, and knead a few minutes. Add a little more flour if it feels sticky.

5. Place in an oiled bowl. Oil the top of the dough, cover the bowl, and let it rise for about an hour until double in size.

6. When it has risen, punch down the dough and make the Butterhorn Rolls on p. 39, Cloverleaf Rolls or Sticky Buns on p. 40, Cinnamon Rolls on p. 41.

Butterhorn Rolls

Makes 24 rolls

1. Prepare:
   Basic Fancy Roll Dough, p. 38

2. Oil 2 cookie sheets.

3. When the dough has doubled, press it down and turn it out on a floured surface. Divide the dough into 2 balls.

4. Roll each half out into a circle with the rolling pin.

5. Spread a little softened margarine or butter on the dough.

6. Cut each circle into 12 wedge-shaped pieces. Pull out the end of each wedge at the broad end, and roll up toward the point. Place on an oiled cookie sheet with the point underneath to prevent unrolling.

7. Brush the tops of the rolls with
   Melted margarine or butter

8. Let rise about 1 hour until very light. Heat the oven to 400°

9. Set the timer for 15 minutes, and bake the rolls in the hot oven until lightly browned.

Cloverleaf Rolls

Makes 24 rolls

1. Prepare the **Basic Fancy Roll Dough,** on p. 38

2. Oil 24 muffin tins.

3. Press down the risen dough. Melt:

   1/2 stick butter or margarine

4. With buttery fingers, pinch off small balls of dough and dip each in melted butter. Put 3 balls in each muffin cup, buttery side up. The cup should be 2/3 full.

5. Let rise until double, about 1 hour. Heat the oven to 400˚.

6. Set the timer for 20 minutes, and bake the rolls in the hot oven.

Sticky Buns

Makes 24 buns

1. Prepare the **Cloverleaf Rolls,** above, up to step 2.

2. After you oil the muffin tins, put on the bottom of each tin:

   1 teaspoon brown sugar

   You can add chopped pecans on top of the sugar, if you want.

3. Continue with the recipe.

4. When the buns are baked, set them upside down on the serving plate.

Cinnamon Rolls

Makes 24 rolls

These rolls rise to fill the pan, so you'll pull apart soft, fragrant buns when they're done baking.

1. After the yeast dough has risen, divide it into 2 balls.

2. Oil the bottoms of two 9 x 9-inch pans, and sprinkle in each:
    1/4 cup brown sugar

3. Roll out each ball into a rectangle about 9 x 12-inches, and spread with:
    2 tablespoons softened margarine

4. Mix together:
    1/2 cup brown sugar
    1 teaspoon cinnamon

5. Sprinkle half the sugar on the first dough rectangle, and roll up, beginning on the longest side. Cut the roll with a knife into 1-inch pieces, and lay the pieces in one of the pans. (It's OK if they touch.)

6. Repeat rolling out the second ball, spreading it with margarine and sprinkling it with the remaining sugar and cinnamon mixture. Roll up, slice, and place the pieces in the second pan.

Gretchen makes Cinnamon Rolls

7. Let the rolls rise about 45 minutes until double in size.

8. Heat the oven to 350°. Set the timer for 25 minutes, and bake until brown.

9. When the pan is removed from the oven, invert it onto a plate while hot, so the rolls won't cool and stick to the bottom of the pan.

Kolacky

Makes 24 rolls

This is a traditional Eastern European recipe (pronounced ko-LATCH-kee).

1. Mix in a small bowl until dissolved:
   1 tablespoon yeast
   1 teaspoon honey or sugar
   1/4 cup warm water

2. Cream together with a slotted spoon in a large bowl:
   1 stick margarine or butter, softened
   2 tablespoons honey or sugar
   1 teaspoon salt

3. Stir in and beat well:
   1 cup warm water
   1 cup flour

4. Add the yeast mixture and stir together well.

5.   Slowly add, while stirring:

3 to 4 cups flour

Use enough flour to make the dough soft, but not sticky.

6.   Turn the dough out onto a floured surface, and knead it a few times. Put it in an oiled bowl, and turn it around to coat with the oil.

7.   Cover the bowl with a clean towel. Set the timer for about 45 minutes, and let the dough rise until doubled in size.

8.   Knead down, pinch off balls the size of a walnut, and place on a lightly oiled baking sheet.

9.   Set the timer for another 30 minutes, and let rise.

10. Heat the oven to 400°. Press down the center of each ball with your thumb to make a small hollow. Fill each hollow with:

1 teaspoon apricot preserves, or

1 teaspoon peach preserves, or

1 teaspoon apple butter

11. When the oven is hot, set the timer for 12 to 15 minutes, and bake the rolls until the tops are lightly browned.

12. Remove from the oven and cool. If desired, sprinkle with powdered sugar.

Vivian cuts parsley to garnish Potato Soup, p. 46.

Soups

Good soup fills up hungry people and homemade soups are the most satisfying. They are easy to make, can be made ahead, and any leftovers are good the next day.

☀ indicates easy-to-make recipe

☀Potato Soup

Makes 6 servings

Potato soup is a great "comfort" food, and easy to prepare too.

1. Heat in a large pan on medium heat:
   6 cups water

2. Prepare and add:
   6 potatoes, peeled and quartered
   1 large onion, peeled and chopped

3. Cover the pan and bring to a boil over high heat. Reduce the heat to low, and cook about 20 to 30 minutes, until the potatoes are fork-tender.

4. With a potato masher, mash the potatoes up into bite-sized chunks.

5. Add to the pan:
   $1/2$ teaspoon salt
   1 cup milk or soymilk
   2 tablespoons margarine or butter

6. Let this heat slowly, but don't let it boil. Ladle the hot soup into bowls, and sprinkle on top:
   $1/2$ cup finely chopped fresh parsley

☀Lentil Soup

Makes 6 servings

Lentils are high in protein, making this a hearty, filling soup.

1. Rinse well and drain in a colander:
    1 pound dry lentils

2. Place in a large pot with:
    8 cups water   **1 bay leaf**

3. Cover the pot and bring to a boil over high heat. Reduce the heat to low, and cook the lentils for 30 minutes.

4. Meanwhile, chop into small pieces:
    2 cloves garlic   **1 large onion**
    2 celery stalks

5. Heat in a frying pan over medium low heat:
    1/4 cup oil

6. Fry the onions and garlic in the oil for 10 minutes. Add the celery and cook 5 minutes more.

7. Add the cooked vegetables to the soup pot, along with:
    1/4 cup tomato sauce or catsup
    1 teaspoon salt   **1/4 teaspoon pepper**

8. Cover the pot and cook over medium heat about 20 minutes more, stirring once in a while. Add more seasonings to taste, if you want. Remove the bay leaf before serving.

☀Vegetable Soup

Makes 8 servings

This is a great way to serve up vegetables, if you have a lot on hand.

1. Slice or chop 2 quarts of fresh vegetables, such as:
    1 large onion, peeled
    1/2 head cabbage
    3 carrots
    4 stalks celery

2. Heat a large, heavy kettle on low. Put in:
    1/4 cup oil

3. Add onions, stir, and cook a few minutes, then add the cabbage. Cook and stir these for 10 minutes.

4. Add the carrots and celery, and cook 10 minutes.

5. Add:
    2 quarts warm water
    1 teaspoon salt
    2 vegetable bouillon cubes, or 2 teaspoons powdered vegetable bouillon

6. Bring to a boil, cover the pan, lower the heat, and simmer about 20 minutes.

Alphabet Soup

1. Prepare:
   Vegetable Soup, p. 48

2. After simmering the soup for 10 minutes, add:
   ½ cup alphabet noodles

3. Cook about 15 minutes more, until the noodles are tender.

Melina cuts napa cabbage
for Vegetable Soup

Croutons

Makes 1 cup

Sprinkle these on soups or salads.

1. Lightly toast, then cut in half-inch cubes:
   3 slices bread

2. Melt in a skillet, then fry cubes in:
   3 teaspoons margarine or butter

3. Stir them as they turn golden brown, then put on a paper towel to drain.

☀Miso Soup With Tofu

Makes 8 servings

Miso tastes a lot like soy sauce, only it's a solid paste. It makes soups, sauces, gravies, and casseroles taste good, but it can be salty, so add a little at a time.

1. Bring to a boil:

    8 cups water

2. Dissolve by stirring together:

    2 tablespoons miso

    1/4 cup warm water

3. Stir the miso mixture into the soup. Don't boil the soup after adding the miso.

4. Cut into small cubes:

    1/2 pound tofu

    Place the tofu in the soup to warm before you ladle the soup into bowls to serve.

5. Chop small:

    3 green onions

    Sprinkle the onions on top of each soup bowl.

☀Rice and Tomato Soup

Makes 6 servings

This is a thick soup; you can add vegetable broth to thin it.

1. In a 2-quart pan over medium heat, melt:
    ½ stick margarine or butter (¼ cup)

2. Add and cook, stirring, for 5 minutes:
    1 cup raw rice

3. Add and cook until soft:
    1 medium onion, peeled and chopped

4. Stir in:
    2 cups fresh or canned tomatoes
    1 teaspoon salt
    4 cups warm water

5. Cover the pan and cook over medium heat until the rice is tender, about 40 minutes.

☀Corn Chowder

Makes 6 servings

Using frozen corn makes this a simple and delicious soup.

1. Chop:
   2 small potatoes
   1 medium onion
   2 stalks celery

2. Heat in a 2-quart pan:
   2 tablespoons vegetable oil

3. Cook the vegetables in the oil for 5 minutes, then add:
   1 tablespoon powdered vegetable bouillon
   4 cups hot water

4. Cover the pan, reduce the heat to low, and cook for 20 minutes.

5. Add to the soup:
   2 cups fresh or frozen corn kernels
   1 cup milk or soymilk

6. Cover and cook 10 minutes more on low heat.

Black Bean Soup

Makes 6 to 8 servings

This can be a meal in itself, with warm Cuban Bread (p. 32) and a salad.

1. Wash and pick out any stones or shriveled beans from:
   1 pound black beans

2. Soak the beans overnight in:
   3 quarts water

3. Drain the beans and add:
   3 quarts fresh water   **1 bay leaf**

4. Bring the beans to a boil over high heat, then reduce the heat to low, cover the pan, and cook 1 to 2 hours, until the beans are tender. To see if the beans are done, squeeze one between your fingers; it should be very soft.

5. Chop up:
   1 large onion   **5 cloves garlic**
   1 green pepper

6. Heat in a heavy skillet:
   1/4 cup olive oil

7. Fry the vegetables until soft. Add to the beans with:
   2 teaspoons cumin   **2 teaspoons oregano**
   1 teaspoon salt   **2 tablespoons vinegar**

8. Simmer together about 30 minutes.

9. Serve over a scoop of **brown rice**, p. 75. Top with chopped red onions, if you like.

Bread Soup

Makes 8 servings

This unusual and tasty soup is a favorite in Europe.

1. Heat a heavy pan, and add:
   2 tablespoons olive oil
   2 medium onions, peeled and chopped

2. Cook for 5 minutes, then sprinkle with:
   1/2 teaspoon salt
   1/4 teaspoon sugar

3. Add:
   1 (15-ounce) can diced tomatoes
   1 clove garlic, chopped
   6 cups vegetable broth

4. Bring to a boil, reduce the heat, cover the pan and simmer for 30 minutes. Have ready:
   8 slices whole wheat bread

5. Heat a skillet and add:
   1 tablespoon oil

6. Fry the bread slices until lightly browned. Ladle the hot soup into bowls, and lay a slice of bread on top of each. Pass grated Parmesan cheese, if desired.

Pea and Barley Soup

Makes 8 servings

This old-fashioned soup tastes wonderful on a cold or rainy day.

1. Rinse and drain:
   2 cups green or yellow dried split peas

2. Place them in a large, heavy kettle with:
   1/3 cup raw pearl barley   **1 carrot, diced**
   1 bay leaf   **8 cups water**

   Bring to a boil, reduce the heat to low, cover the pot, and cook for 30 minutes, stirring a few times.

3. Lightly fry until soft in a small pan:
   2 tablespoons oil
   1 onion, chopped

4. Add the onion to the soup with:
   1 teaspoon salt
   1/2 teaspoon garlic powder
   1/4 teaspoon black pepper

5. Cook another 25 to 30 minutes, tasting to see when barley and peas are tender. Add more seasonings to taste, if you want.

6. Ladle into bowls. You can sprinkle on top:
   Soy "bacon" bits or croutons

☀Minestrone

Makes 6 servings

This is a good way to use up leftover beans or pasta or small amounts of any leftover cooked vegetables. This hearty soup makes a good meal served with salad and Italian bread or rolls.

1. Heat in a heavy 4-quart pot:

   1/4 cup olive oil

   1 onion, peeled and chopped

2. Cook the onion over low heat while you chop:

   2 carrots

   2 stalks celery

3. Add these and cook about 5 minutes, then add:

   3 cups water

   2 cups chopped tomatoes (one 15-ounce can)

   1 teaspoon garlic powder

   1/2 teaspoon salt

4. Cook about 10 minutes, then add:

   2 cups cooked or canned beans

   2 cups cooked pasta

5. Cover and cook about 20 minutes.

6. Ladle the soup into bowls, and serve with a side dish for topping:

   Parmesan cheese or soy Parmesan

Main Dishes

 indicates easy-to-make recipe

Pizza

Makes 4 pizzas (10 inches each)

The best pizza is made with good ingredients. Here's how to make your own pizza easily from scratch, even the crust!

Crust

1. Combine in a large bowl until the yeast has dissolved:

   2 teaspoons dry yeast

   1 teaspoon honey or sugar

   1 cup very warm water

2. Then stir in:

   3 1/2 to 5 cups flour

   1/2 teaspoon salt

   1/4 cup oil

3. Knead the dough in the bowl a few times, then cover it, and let rise for an hour.

4. Punch the dough down and divide into 4 equal-sized balls. Cover them with a towel.

5. On a lightly floured surface, roll each ball out into a 10-inch circle with a floured rolling pin.

6. Lightly oil 2 cookie sheets, and put 2 circles on each. Heat the oven to 425°.

Sauce

1. Mix in a small bowl:

    1 (8-ounce) can tomato paste

    1 (8-ounce) can water

    1 teaspoon basil

    1 teaspoon oregano

Assembly

1. Spread the sauce evenly on the circles.

2. Sprinkle on the toppings of your choice, such as:

    1 large onion, finely chopped

    1 green pepper, finely chopped

    $1/2$ pound mushrooms, sliced

    Black or stuffed olives, sliced

3. Grate and sprinkle on top:

    8 ounces mozzarella cheese or soy mozzarella

4. Set the timer for 15 to 20 minutes, and bake until the cheese is melted and the crust is cooked.

Focaccia

Makes about 18 pieces

You could think of focaccia (fo-KA-sha) as pizza without the tomato sauce.

Crust

1. Make Pizza Crust, p. 58. Roll or pat and stretch to fit into an 11 x 18-inch baking pan with sides. Let rise 30 minutes. While the dough is rising, prepare the topping.

Topping

1. Heat a large skillet over medium-low, and fry, stirring occasionally, until soft:
    2 large onions, chopped
    2 tablespoons olive oil
    1/2 teaspoon salt

2. Spread the cooked onions on top of the dough. Top with:
    1 cup chopped walnuts

    Press down with the back of a spoon.

3. Preheat the oven to 400°, set the timer for 15 minutes, and bake the focaccia. Turn the heat down to 350°, reset the timer for 10 minutes more, and continue to bake.

4. Remove from the oven and cut into strips about 2 inches wide and 5 inches long. Serve warm.

Calzone

Makes 4 calzone

With calzone, the pizza fillings are baked inside the crust.

1. Make one recipe Pizza Crust, p. 58, and let rise until double while you prepare the calzone filling. Heat the oven to 400°.

2. Heat a skillet and slowly fry:

    1 tablespoon olive oil   1 large onion, chopped
    1 green pepper, chopped   1 teaspoon salt

3. Combine in a small bowl:

    1 cup textured soy protein granules (see p. 12)
    $7/8$ cup boiling water

4. Add to the cooked onions:

    1 (8-ounce) can tomato sauce   1 (8-ounce) can sliced black olives
    1 teaspoon basil   1 teaspoon oregano
    The reconstituted granules

5. Divide the pizza dough into 4 balls. Roll each ball out to a circle, and place on an oiled baking pan. Put the filling on half the circle, to within $1/2$ inch of the edge of the dough. Fold the other half of the dough over the filling, and pinch the edges of the dough together to seal. Cut 2 slits, 2 inches long, in the top of each calzone. Brush the tops with olive oil.

6. Set the timer for 20 to 25 minutes, and bake the calzone until the tops are lightly browned.

☀Beans From Scratch

Makes 6 cups

This recipe is good for most beans, such as limas, kidney, white or great Northern beans, and black-eyed peas.

1. Spread out on a plate:
    2 cups dried pinto beans

    Sort out any stones and shriveled beans. Wash the beans well, rinsing in a colander.

2. Add to the beans in a big pot:
    6 cups cold water

    Soak several hours or overnight.

3. Drain the beans. Add fresh water to completely cover them, then add 2 cups more. Then add to the beans, so they won't be gassy:
    1 bay leaf

4. Cover the pot and bring to a boil over high heat. Then reduce the heat to low and cook slowly until tender. This takes 1 to 2 hours. If the water has almost boiled off before the beans are tender, you can add more.

5. To see if the beans are done, squash one between your fingers; it should be very soft. Don't add salt to the beans until they are tender.

Chili

Makes 6 servings

Chili is a vegetarian favorite. If you use textured soy protein granules, your family might not realize they're not eating meat.

1. Measure into a small bowl and stir:
   1 cup textured soy protein (see p. 12)
   ⅞ cup boiling hot water

2. In a 2-quart heavy pan put:
   2 tablespoons oil
   1 medium onion, chopped small
   1 clove garlic, chopped small

3. Fry the onions and garlic over low heat until the onions are soft.

4. Add the reconstituted granules, and fry for 5 minutes.

5. Add to the pan:
   1 (16-ounce) can diced tomatoes (2 cups)
   2 cups water   1 teaspoon cumin powder
   2 tablespoons chili powder   1 teaspoon salt

6. Bring to a boil, reduce the heat, cover, and cook on low for 20 minutes.

7. Break up the tomatoes if they are still in big pieces, then add:
   2 cups cooked pinto or red kidney beans (with their liquid, if canned)

8. Cook for 20 minutes. Taste and add more seasonings, if you like.

☀Chili & Cornbread Topper

Makes 6 servings

This has got to be one of the quickest and easiest meals you can make.

1. Heat the oven to 400°.

2. Heat and pour into an oiled 9 x 13-inch pan:
   1 recipe Chili, p. 63, or 2 (15-ounce) cans chili beans

3. Make according to the directions on the package:
   1 (8-ounce) package cornmeal muffin mix

4. Drop spoonfuls of dough on the chili.

5. Set the timer for 20 minutes, and bake in the hot oven until nicely browned on top.

☀Flour Tortillas

Makes 12 tortillas

Homemade tortillas are delicious. Once you get the hang of rolling them out, you'll find you'll prefer them to store-bought tortillas.

1. Measure into a bowl and stir with a large spoon:

    2 cups flour

    1/2 teaspoon salt

    1 cup water

2. Put a little oil on your hands, and knead the dough a few times. Cover the bowl and let set 15 minutes.

3. Lightly flour a rolling pin and wooden board. Shape the dough into 12 small balls, and flatten each out on the board. Roll into thin circles, turning the dough clockwise as you roll it out to keep it round.

4. When all the tortillas are rolled out, heat a skillet or pancake griddle on medium high.

5. When the griddle is hot, cook each tortilla until barely brown (about 30 seconds). Turn to cook the other side briefly. Brush one side with margarine, butter, or oil, and stack the tortillas up until all are cooked. Cover with a towel to keep them warm and soft.

☀Bean Burritos

Makes 12 burritos

It's so easy to make a complete meal with burritos. You can also add cooked rice, chopped avocado, fried green pepper strips, shredded cabbage, and almost anything else that strikes your fancy.

1. Have ready:

   3 cups cooked pinto beans

   1 red onion, chopped

   2 cups chopped lettuce

   2 tomatoes, diced

   1 cup grated cheese or soy cheese

   Salsa

   Sour cream or soy sour cream (optional)

2. Brown lightly on a greased griddle:

   12 flour tortillas

3. Put a big spoonful of the beans on each tortilla. Let people help themselves to the toppings, and roll their own burritos.

☀Tofu Burritos

Makes 12 burritos

*U*se firm or extra-firm tofu for these, so your filling won't drip out the end of your burrito!

1. You will need:
    12 flour tortillas

2. Mix together in a *medium* bowl:
    1 teaspoon flour
    2 teaspoons chili powder
    1 teaspoon cumin
    1 teaspoon salt
    1/2 teaspoon basil or oregano

    When spices are mixed, crumble in and mix:
    1 pound tofu

3. Heat a heavy skillet on *medium* heat, and add:
    3 tablespoons oil
    The seasoned tofu mix

4. Fry for about 5 minutes, using a pancake turner to keep it from sticking to the pan as it heats.

5. Put the tofu mixture into tortillas, and prepare and serve accompaniments as for Bean Burritos, p. 66.

Enchilada Casserole

Makes 8 servings

A big pan of enchiladas is always a hit and well worth the time it takes to make. Enchiladas are good with the filling for Tofu Burritos too.

You will need:

12 Flour Tortillas, p. 65

6 cups Chili Gravy (see below)

4 cups cooked pinto beans

1 cup grated cheese or soy cheese

Chili Gravy

1. Heat in a heavy 3- or 4-quart pot over low heat:

   1/3 cup vegetable oil

2. Chop and add:

   2 onions

   Fry until the onions are soft.

3. Sprinkle on top of the onion:

   2 tablespoons chili powder

   1 tablespoon cumin powder

   1 teaspoon garlic powder

   1 teaspoon salt

   1/4 teaspoon black pepper

   1/2 cup flour

Stir the flour and seasonings into the onions.

4. Slowly add to the kettle:

    6 cups warm water

Keep stirring with a whisk to work out the lumps as you add the water. Cook this gravy over low heat for 20 minutes, whisking sometimes so it doesn't stick or get lumpy.

Assembly

1. Heat the oven to 350°.

2. Pour into the bottom of an oiled 9 x 13-inch pan:

    2 cups Chili Gravy

3. Heat a heavy skillet or griddle, oil it lightly, and cook the tortillas on each side about 30 seconds.

4. Spread a big spoonful of beans down the middle of each tortilla, roll it up, set it in the gravy in the pan.

5. Continue to cook, fill, and roll until all the tortillas and beans are used.

6. Pour the remaining gravy over the enchiladas.

7. Top the casserole with:

    2 cups grated cheese, soy cheese, or Melty "Cheeze" Sauce, p. 105.

8. Set the timer for 40 minutes, and bake in the hot oven.

9. Cut into squares to serve.

☀Easy Enchiladas

Makes 6 servings

This takes very little time to put together and is a good recipe for beginners or if you are in a hurry.

1. You will need:

   12 corn tortillas

   1 (10-ounce) can enchilada sauce

   2 (15-ounce) cans cooked pinto beans (4 cups)

   1 cup grated cheese, soy cheese, or Melty "Cheeze" Sauce, p. 105

2. Heat the oven to 350°, and oil a 9 x 13-inch pan.

3. Spread half the sauce on the bottom of the pan.

4. Place 6 tortillas on the sauce, overlapping to fit them in the pan.

5. Spread the beans evenly over the tortillas.

6. Place the remaining tortillas on top.

7. Evenly add the rest of the sauce.

8. Top with the grated cheese or cheeze sauce.

9. Set the timer for 40 minutes, and bake in the hot oven.

Quesadillas

Makes 8 servings

This is a popular "fast-food" snack in Mexico.

1. Have ready:

    8 flour tortillas
    1 pound fresh spinach, washed
    1 cup grated Jack cheese or soy Jack cheese

2. Cut the roots and thick stems from the bottoms of the spinach leaves, and chop the leaves in half. Steam or microwave for 2 minutes, then drain.

3. Heat a skillet or griddle, and cook the tortillas one at a time, 30 seconds on a side. Spread a little spinach and about 2 tablespoons of grated cheese on half the tortilla, and fold the other half over. Continue until all the tortillas are filled.

4. Place the filled and folded tortillas back in the hot pan 1 or 2 at a time, and cook about 1 minute on each side, until the cheese melts.

Chili Dogs

Makes 12 dogs

Dough

1. In a large bowl gently stir until the yeast is dissolved:
    1 tablespoon yeast $1/4$ cup warm water
    1 teaspoon honey or sugar

2. Add:
    $3/4$ cup warm water   2 tablespoons oil
    2 cups flour

3. Beat this 100 times, then let it rest for 10 minutes.

4. Beat in:
    1 cup flour
    $1/2$ teaspoon salt

    If dough is sticky, add a little more flour.

5. Pat a little oil on top of the dough, cover the bowl, and let the dough rise in a warm place for one hour.

Chili Filling

1. Measure into a 2-quart bowl:
    1 cup textured soy protein (see p. 12)
    $7/8$ cup boiling water

2. Heat in a heavy 2-quart saucepan:

> 2 tablespoons oil
>
> 1 medium onion, finely chopped
>
> 1 clove garlic, finely chopped

3. Fry the onions and garlic for 5 minutes over medium heat, then add the reconstituted granules, and cook 5 minutes more.

4. Add to the pan:

> 1 (6-ounce) can tomato paste + 1 canful water
>
> 1 teaspoon cumin   1 teaspoon chili powder
>
> 1/2 teaspoon garlic powder   1/2 teaspoon oregano
>
> 1/2 teaspoon salt

5. Cook and stir this mixture for 10 minutes.

Assembly

1. Lightly oil 2 cookie sheets. With oily fingers, press down the dough, and divide into 2 balls.

2. Sprinkle flour on a board and a rolling pin.

3. Lightly roll out 1 ball of dough into a rectangle about 12 inches long.

4. Spread half of the filling mixture on the dough, then roll it the long way. Slice into 6 pieces, and put each slice on the baking sheet. Oil the tops.

5. Repeat with remaining dough and filling.

6. Heat the oven to 350°. Meanwhile, let the chili dogs rise for 10 or 15 minutes on the baking sheet.

7. Set the timer for 25 to 30 minutes, and bake until lightly browned.

"Pigs" In a Blanket

Makes 10 servings

These are perfect to take on a picnic or bring to a pot luck supper.

1. Make the dough for Chili Dogs, p. 72, and let it rise.

2. Open and drain:

   10 vegetarian hot dogs or links

3. Roll half the dough out into a rectangle about 8 x 12 inches. Cut into 5 strips across the short width of the dough. Wrap a strip of dough around each link, starting at one end of the link and making a spiral wrap.

4. Oil a cookie sheet and place the dough-wrapped bundles on it; then roll out the other rectangle, cut 5 more strips, and roll up the remaining "pigs."

5. Heat the oven to 350°. Meanwhile, let the wrapped links rise for 10 to 15 minutes. Set the timer for 25 to 30 minutes, then bake until lightly browned on top.

☀Brown Rice

Makes about 3 cups

We use brown rice in our classes because it's more nutritious than white rice. Serving beans and rice in the same meal give you complete proteins and lots of vitamins and minerals. If you use white rice, it will take less water and a shorter cooking time.

1.   Wash well, then drain in a strainer:

   1 cup brown rice

2.   Put it in a saucepan with a tight-fitting lid. Add:

   2¹/₂ cups water

3.   Bring to a boil, then reduce the heat to a simmer. Cover, set the timer for 40 to 45 minutes, and cook. Remove from the heat and taste a grain to check the tenderness.

☀Rice With Herbs

Makes 6 servings

To add a golden color to this, add 1/2 teaspoon turmeric along with the herbs.

1. Heat in a heavy 2-quart pan over medium:

   3 tablespoons vegetable oil

   1 onion, chopped

   1 cup raw brown rice, washed

2. Fry the onions and rice for about 10 minutes, stirring.

3. Add to the pan:

   2 1/2 cups water

   1 teaspoon salt

   1/2 teaspoon basil

   1/2 teaspoon oregano

   1/2 teaspoon garlic powder

   1/4 teaspoon black pepper

4. Bring to a boil over high heat, then reduce the heat to low. Cover the pan, set the timer for 40 to 45 minutes, and cook until the liquid is absorbed. Turn off the heat and let the rice set on the burner for 10 minutes, covered.

☀Spanish Rice

Makes 6 servings

This dish is so easy, it almost makes itself.

1. Preheat the oven to 350°.

2. Combine in an oiled 2-quart baking dish:

    3¹/₂ to 4 cups cooked brown rice
    1 (4-ounce) can green chiles, drained, seeds removed, and chopped
    1 (15-ounce) can stewed tomatoes

2. Sprinkle the top with:

    paprika

3. Set the timer for about 30 minutes, and bake until piping hot.

Red Beans and Rice

Makes 8 servings

This Louisiana favorite is a delicious way to make beans and rice special.

1. Cook in a saucepan until tender, about 45 minutes:
    1 1/2 cups brown rice
    3 cups water
    1 teaspoon salt

2. Heat a skillet and fry over low heat until soft:
    1 large onion, chopped
    2 tablespoons canola oil

3. Add and stir to combine:
    1/2 teaspoon salt
    1 tablespoon chili powder
    1 teaspoon cumin powder
    1/4 teaspoon garlic powder
    2 (15-ounce) cans red kidney beans, drained

4. Mix the rice, onions, and beans. Cook until hot. Serve with salsa and top with sour cream or soy sour cream.

Fried Rice

Makes 6 servings

Now you can make one of your favorite Chinese dishes right at home.

1. Have ready:
    - 4 cups cooked Brown Rice, p. 75
    - 1 pound firm tofu, cut into small pieces
    - 2 onions, sliced thinly
    - 2 carrots, cut in thin, short sticks
    - 2 stalks celery, sliced thinly

2. Heat in a large skillet or wok:
    - 1/4 cup oil

    Stir in the tofu and vegetables, and fry for about 10 minutes over medium-high heat.

3. Sprinkle on:
    - 1/4 cup soy sauce

4. Break up the cooked rice with a fork, and stir it in.

5. You may add:
    - 1 can sliced water chestnuts, drained
    - Chopped green onions (as garnish)

Chinese Egg Rolls

Makes 20 rolls

These are baked in the oven, not deep fried, and though we make them in quantity they disappear fast! The wrappers or "skins" can be found in the fresh vegetable section of most supermarkets. Frozen tofu works best for these. Defrost a block of tofu frozen overnight, and press out the excess liquid. If you're using fresh tofu, drain it well so the filling isn't too wet.

1. Have ready:

   1 pound tofu, drained, crumbled

   20 egg roll skins or wrappers (one 16-ounce package)

Place the skins under a damp towel after you remove them from the package, so they don't dry out.

Filling:

1. Mix with the tofu:

   2 carrots, grated   2 tablespoons soy sauce
   1/2 teaspoon garlic powder   1/2 teaspoon powdered sugar
   1 teaspoon vinegar

2. Heat a large frying pan, and add:

   1 1/2 cups shredded napa or savoy cabbage
   1/2 cup thinly sliced celery   1 onion, finely chopped
   2 tablespoons oil

3.   Fry the vegetables for about 10 minutes, then add:

    2 tablespoons soy sauce   **2 cups fresh bean sprouts**

4.   Cook a few minutes more, stirring, then add the vegetables to the tofu mixture and mix well.

Assembly:

1.   Oil 2 cookie sheets lightly.

2.   Mix in a cup to make a "paste" for sealing:

    1 tablespoon flour   **1 tablespoon water**

3.   Place a wrapper in front of you like a diamond, and put about $1/3$ cup of filling in the center. Fold over the left side, then the right side, then the top and bottom. Seal the last corner with a little dab of the paste. Set the roll on the oiled cookie sheet with the ends of the wrapper facing down. Lightly oil the top, using a small brush.

4.   Continue filling the wrappers until all are used up. (Any leftover filling is good to eat as is.)

5.   Heat the oven to 400°. Set the timer for 10 minutes, and bake the rolls. Remove the tray from the oven, and turn the rolls over. Return to the oven and bake abut 10 minutes more, until light brown. While the rolls bake, make the dipping sauce to serve on the side.

Dipping Sauce

1.   Mix in a small bowl:

    $1/4$ cup soy sauce   **2 tablespoons vinegar**
    $1/2$ clove garlic, minced

Pot Stickers

Makes 40

1. Cut into 4 quarters to make small squares:
   1 (16-ounce) package egg roll wrappers

 You can freeze any wrappers you will not need to use later. Keep a damp towel on the squares you will use so they do not dry out.

2. Mix in a bowl:
   $1/2$ pound frozen tofu
   2 cups finely chopped cabbage
   $1/2$ cup finely chopped celery
   3 green onions, finely chopped
   1 cup finely chopped mushrooms

3. Stir in:
   2 tablespoons soy sauce
   $1/2$ teaspoon salt
   $1/2$ teaspoon ginger powder

4. Heat a big skillet and stir fry for 5 minutes:
   1 tablespoon canola oil
   The tofu and vegetable mixture

5. Mix in a saucer to make a paste:
   2 teaspoons water
   2 teaspoons flour

6. Take out 1 wrapper square at a time, and put a teaspoon of tofu filling in the center. Gather up the sides to form a bundle, and use a little flour paste to seal the edges together.

7. Heat a big skillet and add, tilting the pan to cover the bottom:

    1 tablespoon oil

Set the pot stickers in the pan carefully in a single layer. (You can use 2 pans or make 2 batches).

8. Cook the potstickers over medium heat for about 3 minutes to brown the bottoms.

9. Carefully add 1 cup water to the pan, avoiding any contact with the steam it creates. Cover the pan, turn the heat to low, and let the dumplings steam for 20 minutes. Most of the liquid will be absorbed.

10. Remove the dumplings to a serving plate. Serve with a dip made by mixing:

    ¹/₄ cup soy sauce

    ¹/₄ cup vinegar

    2 teaspoons crushed gingerroot

Vivian prepares Egg Rolls, p. 80.

Asian Stir Fry

Makes 4 servings

Serve this over hot rice.

1. Heat a big skillet or wok, and fry, stirring continuously, for 1 minute:
   2 tablespoons oil
   1 large onion, cut in half and sliced
   1 large green or red pepper, thinly sliced

2. Add:
   3 carrots, peeled and thinly sliced
   1/2 head cabbage, thinly sliced (about 5 to 6 cups)

Stir well, then turn down the heat to medium. Cook about 5 minutes, until cabbage begins to wilt.

3. Add:
   1 cup thinly sliced celery
   2 tablespoons minced raw gingerroot
   1 teaspoon salt
   1/2 teaspoon sugar
   1/4 cup soy sauce

Stir well, cook 1 more minute, then turn off the heat and serve immediately.

☀Barbecued Tofu

Makes 3 to 4 servings

Barbecued tofu is so delicious, you may want to make twice as much just to be sure you'll have enough for seconds.

1. Heat the oven to 350°.

2. Wrap in a towel for a few minutes to dry:
   1 pound firm or extra-firm tofu

3. Cut into 12 or 14 slices, and place on an oiled baking pan.

4. Spread each slice with:
   Your favorite barbecue sauce

5. Set the timer for 10 minutes, and bake the tofu; then turn the slices over, reset the timer for 10 minutes more, and bake the other side.

Tofu Pot Pie

Makes 6 to 8 servings

Vegetables in a yummy gravy under a pastry crust, baked to a golden brown, makes a wonderful dinner. Thaw frozen tofu before you start, or use fresh tofu.

Filling

1. Prepare:
   3 medium potatoes, peeled and cut into chunks
   3 carrots, peeled and thinly sliced

2. Heat to boiling:
   4 cups water

   Add the potatoes and cover. Set the timer for 10 minutes and cook.

3. Add the sliced carrots to the potatoes. Cook until the potatoes are fork-tender. Drain, saving the liquid to use in the gravy, and set aside.

Gravy

1. Heat a heavy 4-quart pot, and add:
   1/4 cup oil
   1 large onion, chopped

   Cook over low heat until soft.

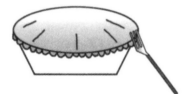

2. Add to the onions and cook a few minutes more:
   1/2 cup sliced celery

3. Press the liquid from:

    1 pound defrosted tofu

    Cut or tear it into bite-sized pieces.

4. Sprinkle the tofu with:

    2 tablespoons soy sauce

5. Mix in well. Add to the pan and stir in:

    $^1/_3$ cup flour

6. Measure the potato liquid into a 1-quart measure, and add enough water to make 4 cups. Pour into the pan and stir well.

7. Add as you cook and stir the gravy:

    $^1/_2$ teaspoon garlic powder   **$^1/_2$ teaspoon thyme**

    $^1/_2$ teaspoon oregano   **$^1/_2$teaspoon black pepper**

    2 teaspoons powdered vegetable bouillon

8. Cook the gravy for 10 minutes, then add the potatoes and carrots. Taste the gravy and add more seasonings if you like.

9. Pour the filling into a round 2-quart baking dish. The dish should be 9 or 10 inches wide.

Pastry Crust and Assembly

1. Preheat the oven to 400°.

2. Using a pastry blender, mix until it looks like crumbs:

    2 cups flour   **$^1/_2$ teaspoon salt**

    $^3/_4$ stick margarine or butter, or $^2/_3$ cup oil

3. Work in with a fork, to make a ball of dough:

    2 to 3 tablespoons ice water

4.   On a lightly floured surface, pat and roll the dough into a circle 1 inch bigger all around than the top of your baking dish. Carefully fold the pastry in half, and then in half again, so you can lift the pastry up and lay it on top of the pie filling. Unfold it to cover the pie. Turn the edges under neatly, then go around the rim of the crust with the tines of a fork, pressing the edges down to seal. (See the drawing on page 86.)

5.   Make six 2-inch slashes in the crust with a knife to let the steam escape while baking.

6.   Set the pie on a baking sheet, as it may bubble over. Set the timer for 30 minutes, and bake until the top is lightly browned.

Ben tops Lasagne, p. 93, with cheese.

Baked Tofu

Makes 3 to 4 servings

Nutritional yeast flakes give a golden color and add a rich flavor to this.

1. Wrap in a towel to drain:
    1 pound tofu

2. Mix for a marinade in a shallow pan:

    1 cup water   **2 tablespoons soy sauce**

    1 teaspoon thyme   **1 teaspoon marjoram**

    1 tablespoon nutritional yeast flakes (see p. 12)

3. Cut the tofu into 12 slices. Put them in the marinade, and let soak for 10 minutes. Then heat oven to 350°.

4. Mix for a breading on a plate:

    1/2 cup flour

    2 tablespoons nutritional yeast flakes

    1 teaspoon salt

    1 teaspoon paprika

5. Dip the tofu slices into the breading, and lay them out on a large, oiled baking sheet.

6. Set the timer for 10 minutes, and bake the tofu. Turn the slices over, reset the timer for 10 minutes again, and bake the other side.

☀Noodle Casserole

Makes 8 servings

1. Bring to a boil over high heat in a large kettle:
   3 quarts water
   1 teaspoon salt

2. Add and stir a few times with a big wooden spoon until the water boils again
   1 pound medium flat noodles

3. Set the timer for about 8 minutes, and continue to stir. Taste a noodle to be sure it is cooked. Pour the noodles into a colander to drain, and cover with a towel so they don't dry out.

4. While the noodles are cooking, put into a large bowl:
   1 stick margarine, melted   **1 teaspoon garlic powder**
   4 green onions, chopped   **1/4 cup finely chopped parsley**
   1 pound firm tofu, crumbled, or 2 cups of cottage cheese

5. Heat the oven to 350°. Oil a 3-quart casserole.

6. Mix the cooked noodles into the bowl with the melted margarine or butter, stir well, then stir in:
   1/4 cup Parmesan cheese or soy Parmesan
   1/2 cup sour cream or soy sour cream
   1/4 teaspoon black pepper

7. When the noodles and sauce are well mixed, put them in the oiled casserole and cover with foil. Set the timer for 25 minutes, and bake in the hot oven.

Macaroni and Cheese

Makes 4 to 6 servings

This is so much tastier than anything you'll make from a package.

1. Make a white sauce by combining in a 2-quart pan over low heat:

   1/2 stick margarine

   1/4 cup flour

   1/2 teaspoon salt

2. When the flour mixture bubbles, slowly stir in:

   2 cups milk or soymilk

3. Cook and stir the sauce until it is thick and begins to bubble. Remove from the heat and stir in:

   1 to 2 cups grated Jack or cheddar cheese, grated soy Jack or cheddar, or Melty "Cheeze" Sauce, p. 105

4. Cook in 2 quarts boiling water, then drain.

   8 ounces elbow macaroni

5. Heat the oven to 375°. Add the drained macaroni to the cheese sauce.

6. Oil a 9 x13 x 2-inch pan. Pour in the macaroni and sauce, and top with:

   1/2 cup crushed crackers or bread crumbs

7. Set the timer for 30 minutes, and bake until bubbly.

☀Italian Pasta Sauce

Makes 4 cups

1. Cook in a heavy 2-quart pan over low heat until soft:

   ¹/₄ cup oil   **1 large onion, finely chopped**

2. Stir in:

   1 (17-ounce) can tomato purée   **1 teaspoon oregano**

   2 teaspoons basil   **1 teaspoon garlic powder**

3. Mix in a bowl, then add:

   2 teaspoons powdered vegetable bouillon

   2 cups hot water

4. Cook over low heat for 20 to 30 minutes, stirring occasionally.

5. Serve the sauce on the cooked, drained pasta and pass a dish of:

   Grated Parmesan cheese, grated soy Parmesan, or nutritional yeast flakes

☀Mushroom Pasta Sauce

Makes 3 to 4 servings

1. Wash, dry on paper towels, and chop:

   8 ounces fresh mushrooms

2. Melt in a large skillet over medium heat:

   2 tablespoons butter or margarine

3. Add the mushrooms and stir-fry until lightly browned. Then add the mushrooms with their liquid to the pasta sauce.

☀Lasagne

6 servings

Kids are pleased to find that this favorite dish is not hard to make. No need to cook noodles first; just layer them right out of the package.

1. Have ready:

    4 cups Italian Pasta Sauce, p. 92, or 1 (32-ounce) jar pasta sauce

    1/2 pound lasagne noodles (9 large noodles)

    15 ounces ricotta cheese, or 1 pound tofu, well-drained and crumbled

    1/2 pound mozzarella cheese or soy mozzarella, grated, or 2 cups Melty "Cheeze" Sauce, p. 105

2. Heat the oven to 350°.

3. Put a little of the sauce in the bottom of an oiled 9 x 13-inch pan that is at least 2 inches deep.

4. Layer half the noodles on the sauce.

5. Dot the noodles with spoonfuls of the ricotta or tofu.

6. Sprinkle on half the mozzarella cheese or cheeze sauce.

7. Spread with half the remaining sauce.

8. Make another layer of noodles, then the rest of the ricotta or tofu, then the rest of the sauce, and top with the last of the cheese. Cover the pan with aluminum foil.

9. Set the timer for 45 minutes, and bake in the hot oven.

10. Remove the foil, reset the timer for 15 minutes, and continue to bake. Cool for 5 or 10 minutes before cutting into squares to serve.

Stuffed Shells

Makes 6 servings

If you have fresh basil or oregano, use twice as much. Shells are terrific with fresh herbs in the filling.

Tomato Sauce

1. Heat a heavy 2-quart pan, and cook on low heat for 10 minutes:
   2 tablespoons olive oil
   1 onion, chopped

2. Add to the pan:
   1 (6-ounce) can tomato paste
   2 cans water
   1/2 teaspoon salt
   1/2 teaspoon dried basil
   1/2 teaspoon dried oregano
   1/2 teaspoon garlic powder

3. Cook the sauce for about 20 minutes, stirring a few times.

Shells

1. Bring to a boil in a large pot:
   3 quarts water

2. Add (while handling gently):
   18 large shells

Boil about 15 minutes, until the shells are tender. Stir them several times with a big wooden spoon to be sure they don't stick together.

3.   Drain the shells in a colander, then put them back in the pan. Put cold water over the shells in pan so they don't dry out. Handle shells gently so they don't break while you stuff them.

Filling for Shells

1.   Mix together in a bowl:

1 pound fresh tofu, crumbled	1/4 cup olive oil
2 tablespoons chopped parsley	1 teaspoon oregano
1 teaspoon basil	1/2 teaspoon garlic powder
1/2 teaspoon salt	

Assembly

1.   Heat the oven to 350°. Oil a 9 x 13-inch pan.

2.   Put 1 cup of sauce in the bottom of the pan.

3.   Stuff the shells with the filling and place in the pan. Spoon the remaining sauce over the shells.

4.   Sprinkle the top with:

   1/2 cup grated Parmesan cheese, grated soy Parmesan, or Melty "Cheeze" Sauce, p. 105

5.   Set the timer for 30 minutes, and bake in the hot oven.

Falafel

Makes 24 balls

1. Heat the oven to 350°.

2. Mash together:

   2 (15-ounce) cans chick-peas (garbanzo beans), drained, or 3 to 3^1/$_2$ cups cooked, drained beans

   ^{1}/$_4$ cup whole wheat flour

   2 tablespoons wheat germ

   ^{1}/$_4$ cup minced onion

   2 tablespoons minced fresh parsley

   1 tablespoon soy sauce

   1 teaspoon paprika

   ^{1}/$_4$ teaspoon garlic powder

3. With wet hands, shape the mixture into 1-inch balls.

4. Place the balls on a greased baking sheet. Set the timer for 15 minutes, and bake. Then turn the falafel over, reset the timer for 5 minutes, and bake a little longer. Instead of baking these, you can fry them in a little oil in a hot skillet.

5. Serve falafel in pita breads cut in half along with:

   Sour cream or soy sour cream

   Chopped fresh tomatoes or salsa.

☀World's Fair Specials

Makes 5 servings

We stood in line at the World's Fair in Knoxville, Tennessee, in 1982 to buy little dishes of this delicious combination.

1. Have ready:

    2 (16-ounce) cans chili beans

    1 onion, chopped

    2 tomatoes, chopped

    1 cup grated Jack cheese or soy Jack cheese

    2 cups chopped lettuce

    1 cup sour cream or soy sour cream

    1 (6-ounce) jar salsa or picante sauce

    1 (12-ounce) bag corn chips

2. Heat the beans in a small saucepan on medium heat. Arrange the toppings in bowls.

3. Put a handful of chips on each plate. Top with a big spoonful of beans, and let everyone help themselves to the toppings.

☀Easy "Sausage" Balls

Makes 48 balls

This is one of the recipes that the kids wanted to make again and again. If the tempeh is frozen, let it defrost completely before steaming.

1. Steam in a steamer for 15 minutes:

   8 ounces tempeh (see p. 12)

   Let cool after steaming.

2. In a large bowl, sift together:

   3 cups flour   **4 teaspoons baking powder**
   1 teaspoon salt

3. Using a pastry blender, cut in until it looks like coarse crumbs:

   1 stick margarine or butter

4. Grate the tempeh (use the large holes of the grater); add to the flour mixture.

5. Sprinkle in:

   1 teaspoon thyme   **1 teaspoon oregano**
   1 teaspoon sage   **1/3 cup Parmesan cheese or soy Parmesan**

   Mix the flour, tempeh, and seasonings together.

6. Stir in:

   1/2 cup milk or soymilk

7. Preheat the oven to 375°. Lightly oil 2 cookie sheets.

8. With oily fingers, shape pieces of dough into balls the size of a walnut. The mixture will make about 48 balls. Place them on the oiled cookie sheets.

9. Set the timer for 25 minutes, and bake in the hot oven until lightly browned. Remove from the oven, and serve warm as a snack, or with Golden Gravy, p. 99 as a main dish.

☀Golden Gravy

Makes 2 cups

This is delicious served on rice or biscuits. Serve over rice, potatoes, biscuits, or "Sausage" Balls, p. 98.

1. Toast in a 6-cup heavy-bottomed saucepan over medium low for about 10 minutes, stirring it a few times:

   1/3 cup flour

2. Add:

   1/3 cup nutritional yeast flakes (see p. 12)

   Stir and toast the flour and yeast 3 minutes more.

3. Add:

   1/4 cup canola oil

4. Whisk the oil and flour together.

5. Stir together in a small pan:

   2 cups hot water

   2 teaspoons powdered vegetable bouillon

6. Slowly whisk the liquid into the flour mix, and keep whisking to make the gravy smooth. Cook a few minutes, as it thickens and bubbles.

7. Whisk in:

   2 tablespoons soy sauce or a pinch of salt

   Taste and add more seasoning, if you like.

Knishes

Makes 16 knishes

Both the dough and filling in this recipe use mashed potatoes. You can also try a filling of kasha (buckwheat groats), p. 102.

Dough

1. Peel and cut into quarters:

   4 large potatoes

   Cover with water in a saucepan, and simmer until soft.

2. Drain the potatoes, put back into the pan, and mash with:

   ¼ stick margarine or butter
   ¼ cup milk or soymilk
   1 teaspoon salt

3. Stir in a large bowl:

   3 cups flour
   2 teaspoons baking powder
   1 tablespoon oil
   1 cup mashed potatoes
   ½ cup cold water

   Set aside the remaining potatoes for the filling.

4. Use your hand to knead the dough until smooth. Cover the bowl and let the dough rest for 30 minutes while you mix the filling.

Filling

1. Fry in a heavy pan until tender:
    2 tablespoons oil
    1 large onion, chopped

2. Add the onion to the mashed potatoes set aside for the filling, along with:
    1 cup crumbled tofu, or 1 cup cottage cheese, drained
    ¹/₂ teaspoon garlic powder
    ¹/₂ teaspoon thyme
    ¹/₄ teaspoon pepper
    ¹/₄ cup chopped fresh parsley

Assembly

1. Heat the oven to 375°. Oil a baking sheet.

2. Separate the dough into 4 balls. On a lightly floured board, roll out a ball into a square, about ¹/₃-inch thick. Cut into 4 smaller squares.

3. Put 2 to 3 tablespoons of filling in the center of a square, and fold the dough over the filling. Repeat for all the dough.

4. Place the knishes on the oiled pan. Set the timer for 25 minutes, and bake until golden.

 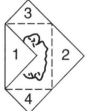 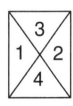

Kasha

Makes 6 servings

When kasha is cooked, it can be mixed with cooked bow-tie pasta as a main dish or used as a filling for knishes.

1. Mix with a fork in a small bowl:

    1 cup kasha (roasted buckwheat groats)

    1 egg*

2. Heat in a large pan:

    2 tablespoons margarine or butter

    Add the kasha and cook, stirring, until it is light brown and crumbly.

3. Heat to boiling in another pan:

    2 cups water

4. Carefully add the boiling water to the kasha, standing back to avoid the steam. Stir well, cover the pan, and cook over low heat for about 15 minutes.

5. Meanwhile, fry in a heavy skillet on medium heat:

    2 tablespoons oil

    1 large onion, finely chopped

6. Fluff the kasha with a fork, and stir in the fried onions.

    *Vegan Alternative: Omit the egg and go on to the next step.

Boofers

Makes 6 servings

You can use instant mashed potatoes in these, but reduce the water normally added to the potato flakes by 1/3 so they aren't too soft to shape into patties.

1. Scrub well and cook in enough water to cover:

   6 potatoes, cut in half

2. Cook 30 minutes, or until fork-tender. While the potatoes are cooking, fry over low heat:

   1 tablespoon margarine or butter

   1 small onion, chopped

3. Drain the potatoes in a colander. Put in a large bowl, and mash, adding:

   1/2 stick margarine or butter

   1 teaspoon salt

   The fried onions

4. Add:

   1 pound tofu, drained and crumbled

   1/4 cup chopped fresh parsley

5. Shape into 12 patties about 1/2-inch thick as soon as the mixture is cool enough to handle.

6. Heat a pancake griddle or heavy skillet on medium-high, and oil the surface.

7. Fry the boofers until nicely browned on the bottom. Carefully turn over and brown the other side, keeping the griddle oiled so the boofers don't stick.

☀Nacho Pie

Makes 6 servings

1. Heat in a 2-quart pan:

   2 (16-ounce) cans pinto beans, or 4 cups cooked pinto beans with a little of their cooking liquid

2. When the beans are hot, remove from the stove, and add:

   1 teaspoon chili powder

   1 teaspoon cumin powder

   1 teaspoon garlic powder

   1 teaspoon oregano

   1/4 teaspoon black pepper

3. Mash the beans well. Taste and add more seasoning, if you like. Put the beans back on the stove, and cook over low heat, stirring so they don't stick, until most of the liquid has cooked away. Taste again for seasonings.

4. Heat the oven to 350˚.

5. Oil a 9-inch pie pan, and spread the beans in the pan.

6. Stick into the beans:

   30 tortilla chips

7. Sprinkle on top:

   1 cup grated cheese or soy cheese

8. Set the timer for 15 minutes, and bake in the hot oven.

Melty "Cheeze" Sauce

Makes 2¹/₂ cups

W̲e make this *yummy* sauce with good tasting nutritional yeast that comes in yellow flakes and adds a nutty, cheezy flavor to spreads, sauces, breading mixes, and popcorn.

1. Mix in a 1-quart saucepan:

   ¹/₂ cup nutritional yeast flakes (p. 12)

   ¹/₂ cup cornstarch

   2 tablespoons flour

   1 teaspoon salt

2. Whisk in:

   2 cups water

   ¹/₂ cup canola oil

   1 teaspoon wet mustard

3. Cook and stir until the sauce thickens and bubbles. It will get thicker as it cooks and can be thinned down with a little more water..

Sam arranges tortilla chips to top a Nacho Pie, p. 104.

Sam and Gretchen fix vegetables for Tossed Salad Greens, p. 108.

Salads & Dressings

☀ indicates easy-to-make recipe

☀Tossed Salad Greens

Makes 6 servings

Try using the wide variety of salad greens that are available in supermarkets these days. If you've eaten mostly head lettuce, you'll be surprised at the many tasty flavors salad greens can have.

1. Wash and drain in a colander:

    2 quarts fresh salad greens, such as lettuce, romaine, spinach

    Gently pat dry on a clean towel.

2. Tear the greens into a salad bowl. Add fresh vegetables, such as:

    Tomatoes, sliced or chunked

    Cucumbers, sliced

    Carrots, grated

    Onions or avocados, sliced

    Red or green pepper strips

    Fresh raw mushrooms, rinsed, dried, and sliced

3. Using a big spoon and fork, toss the salad with enough dressing to lightly coat the greens, about two or three tablespoons. Don't use too much.

4. Nice toppers on a tossed salad are:

    Soy "bacon" bits

    Croutons, p. 49

    Grated Parmesan, soy Parmesan, or crumbled feta cheese

Macaroni Salad

Makes 8 servings

Other kinds of pasta beside macaroni can be used in this salad. Try small shells or spirals (rotelle). Follow directions on package for cooking the pasta.

1. Heat in a large pot until boiling:

   3 quarts water

2. Add and boil 8 to 10 minutes:

   2 cups elbow macaroni

   1 teaspoon salt

   Stir a few times with a wooden spoon so the macaroni doesn't stick to the bottom of the pan. Taste a piece to make sure it is tender. Drain the pasta in a colander.

3. Mix in a large serving bowl:

   2 tablespoons oil

   2 tablespoons vinegar

4. Add the drained pasta and stir with a big spoon. Cover the bowl and chill the macaroni.

5. When chilled, add:

   3 green onions, chopped   **1 cup finely chopped celery**

   2 carrots, grated

6. Mix the macaroni with the vegetables, and add:

   3 tablespoons mayonnaise or soy mayonnaise

   3 tablespoons sour cream or soy sour cream

You can also use only mayonnaise, enough to moisten. Taste and add a little salt and a few dashes of pepper, if you like. Chill the salad until serving time.

☀ Tofu Salad

Makes 4 servings

This is the vegetarian equivalent of egg salad.

1. Drain in a colander:
    1 pound fresh tofu

2. Prepare these vegetables:
    2 green onions, thinly sliced
    2 stalks celery, finely chopped
    1 medium carrot, grated

3. Using the large holes of the grater, grate the tofu, or crumble it into a bowl.

4. Mix together the tofu and vegetables. Stir in:
    1/4 cup mayonnaise or soy mayonnaise

    You may want to add either:
    Chopped fresh herbs, or pickle relish

5. Taste and add as needed:
    Salt and pepper

    Serve the salad on lettuce leaves, or use as a filling for sandwiches.

☀Cucumber Salad

Makes 6 servings

This mixture makes good sandwiches. Try it on rye or French bread.

1. Slice thinly into a medium bowl:
   2 medium cucumbers

2. Sprinkle with:
   1 teaspoon salt

   Cover the bowl and chill 30 minutes.

3. Rinse and drain the cucumbers, pressing out the excess liquid.

4. Mix in:
   1/2 cup tofu sour cream
   2 teaspoons dill weed

   Chill for 30 minutes or more to blend the flavors.

5. Stir well before serving.

☀Potato Salad

Makes 6 servings

Potato salad is such a welcome favorite. Start with this recipe and vary it to suit your particular tastes.

1. Heat in a large pot on medium-high:

   2 quarts water

2. Meanwhile, scrub well or peel, then cut into quarters:

   6 potatoes

   Add to the pot, set the timer for 20 to 30 minutes, and cook until they are fork-tender.

3. Drain the potatoes in a colander and put into a bowl. Cover and cool before dicing.

4. Meanwhile, prepare:

   1/4 cup finely chopped onion   **1 carrot, peeled and grated**
   1/2 cup thinly sliced celery   **1/4 cup finely chopped fresh parsley**

5. Cut the potatoes into smaller pieces, mix with the vegetables and add:

   1/2 cup or more mayonnaise or soy mayonnaise, enough to moisten.

   Taste and add a little salt and pepper, if you like, along with:

   1 tablespoon wet mustard, or 1 tablespoon pickle juice

6. Chill the salad. Before serving, decorate the top with one or more of these:

   Wedges of tomato   **Sliced radishes**
   Slices of pickle   **Wedges of hard-boiled eggs**

Coleslaw

Makes 6 servings

You could experiment with different types of salad dressings and have a different coleslaw every time you made it.

1. Shred, thinly slice, or chop up:

    4 cups cabbage

    Don't use the tough outer leaves.

2. Prepare:

    2 carrots, grated

    3 green onions, sliced, or 1 medium onion, chopped small

3. Mix together, then stir in about:

    1/2 cup of your favorite dressing, or Honey Dressing, p. 120

    Use more or less, as you like it. Taste and add a little salt and pepper.

4. Chill well before serving.

Pineapple Cabbage Salad

Makes 8 servings

Try this for a winter salad when you want something different.

1. Drain:

   1 (8-ounce) can pineapple tidbits

   (You can drink the juice.)

2. Chop or shred:

   4 cups cabbage

3. Mix the cabbage and pineapple.

4. Mix with a fork in a small bowl:

   $1/2$ cup plain yogurt
   2 tablespoons mayonnaise or soy mayonnaise

5. Stir this dressing into the salad. Taste and add salt if you like.

Spicy Noodle Salad

Makes 8 servings

If you like Thai food (or have been wanting to try some), this salad should fill the bill.

1. Bring to a boil in a large pot:

    2 quarts water

2. Add and cook for 6 or 7 minutes, until the noodles are tender:

    1 pound angel hair pasta
    1 teaspoon salt

Drain in a colander and run cold water over the noodles.

3. Put the drained noodles in a bowl, and toss gently with:

    2 teaspoons toasted sesame oil

4. Add to the noodles, mixing gently:

    2 carrots, peeled, grated   **1 cup finely chopped celery**
    3 green onions, finely chopped   **1 tablespoon minced raw gingerroot**
    1/4 cup finely chopped fresh cilantro

4. Stir together for a dressing:

    1 tablespoon peanut butter   **2 tablespoons cider vinegar**
    2 tablespoons soy sauce
    1/4 teaspoon crushed red pepper flakes

5. Stir the dressing into the noodles and vegetables, and keep the salad cold until serving time.

Tempuna Salad

Makes 6 servings

This makes a delicious sandwich filling.

1. Put a steamer basket in a saucepan with a tightly fitting lid. Add water almost to the bottom of the basket. Heat to a simmer. Put in basket:

   8 ounces tempeh, defrosted if frozen (p. 12)

   Cover, set the timer for 15 minutes, and steam. Remove the tempeh from the pan, and cool.

2. Meanwhile, chop up:

   1 small onion
   2 stalks celery
   2 tablespoons fresh parsley
   1/4 cup pickles

3. Grate the tempeh into a medium bowl, using the large holes on the grater.

4. Mix together the tempeh and vegetables with:

   Enough mayonnaise to moisten

   Taste the salad and add salt and pepper if you like.

5. Chill. Serve on lettuce or in sandwiches.

☀Summer Fruit Salad

Makes 6 servings

A fruit salad is always the number one favorite in hot weather. This can be served on lettuce as a first course, with or without Celery Seed Salad Dressing, p. 122.

1. Prepare 5 or 6 cups of fresh fruit, such as:

   2 cups cubed watermelon

   1 cup diced cantaloupe

   1 cup blueberries, washed and drained

   1 cup hulled, sliced strawberries

   1 cup peeled, sliced peaches

   1 apple, cut in small pieces

You can use varying amounts of any fruits available. Mix the fruits together in a bowl, then chill.

Ambrosia

Makes 4 servings

Shredded coconut is what makes this more than just fruit salad.

1. Put into a medium bowl:
   2 oranges, peeled and cut up
   2 bananas, sliced

2. Cut up and add:
   1 small (8-ounce) can pineapple slices with their juice

3. Mix well. Spoon into serving dishes. You may sprinkle on top of each:
   1 tablespoon shredded coconut

Apple Walnut Salad

Makes 6 servings

This is our version of Waldorf salad, made famous by a chef at the Waldorf-Astoria Hotel in New York in the 1890s.

1. Core and cut up:

    4 medium apples

2. Mix with:

    1/2 cup finely chopped celery
    1/2 cup finely chopped walnuts

3. Combine in a small bowl:

    1/4 cup mayonnaise or soy mayonnaise
    1 teaspoon honey or sugar
    1 tablespoon lemon juice
    1/2 teaspoon celery salt

4. Mix together with the apples, celery, and walnuts. Cover and chill until serving time.

Tofu Dressing

Makes about 1¹/₃ cups

Your can start with this basic recipe and add herbs, garlic, miso, nutritional yeast flakes, and other flavorings.

1. Combine in a food processor or blender:

    ¹/₂ **pound soft tofu, crumbled**   ¹/₄ **cup oil**

    2 **tablespoons lemon juice**   ¹/₄ **teaspoon salt**

2. Whip until smooth and creamy, scraping down sides of the blender or processor when the motor is off.

☀Honey Dressing

Makes about ³/₄ cup

This is particularly good in coleslaw.

1. Shake together in a jar:

    ¹/₄ **cup vinegar**   2 **tablespoons honey**

    ¹/₂ **teaspoon salt**   ¹/₈ **teaspoon pepper**

    ¹/₂ **teaspoon celery seed**   ¹/₃ **cup vegetable oil**

☀French Dressing

Makes 1/2 cup

This is a classic dressing that's good to know how to make.

1. Put into a small jar:

   1/4 cup vinegar

   1/4 teaspoon salt

   6 tablespoons canola oil

   1 teaspoon honey or sugar

   1/4 teaspoon paprika

2. Shake well. Keep in a covered jar.

☀Thousand Island Dressing

Makes 1 cup

This is also good as a sandwich spread.

1. Mix in a small bowl:

   1 cup mayonnaise or soy mayonnaise

   2 tablespoons chili sauce or ketchup

   1 teaspoon grated onion

   2 tablespoons stuffed olives, finely chopped

   1 hard boiled egg, finely chopped (optional)

2. Serve on lettuce, sliced tomatoes, or a salad of mixed greens.

Celery Seed Salad Dressing

Makes about 2 cups

This creamy dressing must be made in a blender or food processor. If you use a blender, be sure to stop the machine every minute or so and push down the sides with a rubber scraper.

1. Crumble into a blender or food processor

    1 cup (¹/₂ pound) tofu

2. Add:

    ¹/₂ cup canola oil

    ¹/₂ cup sugar

    ¹/₂ teaspoon salt

    1 tablespoon celery seed

    1 teaspoon wet yellow mustard

    ¹/₂ teaspoon paprika

3. Pulse the blender or processor on and off, scraping down the sides, until the dressing is creamy and well mixed.

4. Pour into a small pitcher for serving, and keep chilled.

Herb Dressing

Makes 3/4 cup

Be creative. If you have fresh herbs, use them, but use twice as much. Any remaining dressing will keep for days in a covered jar.

1. In a small jar with a tightly fitting lid, shake up:

   1/4 cup vinegar

   1/2 teaspoon salt

   1/4 teaspoon dry mustard

   1/4 teaspoon pepper

   1/2 cup olive oil

2. Add 1 teaspoon of one of these herbs for flavor:

   Dill weed

   Basil

   Oregano

   Any herb or combination

Sam cuts up apples for Apple Crisp, p. 126.

Desserts

☀ indicates easy-to-make recipe

☀Apple Crisp

Makes 6 servings

The rolled oats you use in this recipe is the same as long-cooking oatmeal (not the instant kind).

1. Oil an 8 x 8-inch pan. Heat the oven to 350°.

2. Slice into the pan:

   6 apples

3. Mix together in a bowl:

   1/2 stick margarine or butter

   1/3 cup sugar

   1/3 cup flour

   1 cup rolled oats

4. Spread this crumbly mixture over the apples.

5. Set the timer for 40 to 45 minutes, and bake the apples until you can stick a fork through them easily.

☀Apple Cake

Makes 6 servings

This makes a delicious breakfast cake, as well as a dessert.

1. Oil an 8 x 8-inch pan. Heat the oven to 350°.

2. Stir together:
    3/4 cup sugar
    1 cup flour
    2 teaspoons baking powder

3. Add and mix well:
    1/2 cup water
    2 tablespoons oil
    1 teaspoon vanilla

4. Add to the batter:
    2 apples, peeled and cut up
    1/2 cup chopped walnuts

5. Pour into the oiled pan. Set the timer for 35 to 40 minutes, and bake. Cool and cut into squares to serve.

Applesauce

Makes about 2 cups

1. Wash and cut into quarters, removing the cores:
   3 large or 4 medium apples

2. Put them in a pan with:
   1/2 cup water

3. Cover and cook slowly until tender, about 15 minutes. Stir now and then.

4. Mash the apples with a potato masher, and taste, adding a little honey or sugar if desired. If you use a sweet apple like Golden Delicious, you may not want to add any additional sweetener.

5. Sprinkle with:
   Cinnamon

Tofu Whipped Topping

Makes 1 cup

1. Combine in a blender or food processor:
   1/2 pound tofu, crumbled   **1/4 cup canola oil**
   3 tablespoons sugar   **1 teaspoon vanilla**
   1/4 teaspoon salt

2. Blend until smooth. Pour into a bowl, and chill.

☀Caramel Fried Apples

Makes 6 servings

A bowl of these makes a great after-school snack.

1. Cut each into 8 pieces, removing the seeds and cores:
    6 apples

2. Melt together over medium-low heat in a big skillet or wok:
    $1/2$ stick margarine or butter
    $1/2$ cup sugar

3. Cook the mixture slowly for 5 minutes to make a syrup.

4. Lay the apples in the skillet, being careful not to burn your fingers. Spoon the syrup over the top of the apples.

5. Cover the pan, set the timer for 10 minutes, and cook on low heat until the apples are tender-crisp.

☀Gram's Peach Cobbler

6 servings

This batter is good on other fruit too. Try it with blackberries or strawberries.

1. Oil an 8 x 8-inch pan. Heat the oven to 350°.

2. Slice into the pan:

   6 fresh peaches, peeled and pitted.

3. Sprinkle them with:

   1/4 cup sugar

4. Using a whisk, beat until foamy in a medium bowl:

   2 eggs*

5. Add to the eggs:

   2 tablespoons water
   2 tablespoons sugar
   2/3 cup flour
   1 teaspoon baking powder

6. Mix the batter well with the whisk. Pour the batter over the peaches, set the timer for 30 minutes, and bake until the top is lightly browned. Serve warm.

*Vegan Alternative: Instead of 2 eggs, you can use 1 tablespoon Ener-G Egg replacer mixed with 1/4 cup water.

☀Baked Bananas

Makes 4 servings

You can get green bananas to ripen more quickly by storing them in a paper bag for a day or two.

1. Heat the oven to 350˚.

2. Spread the bottom of an 8 x 8-inch baking dish with margarine or butter.

3. Peel and cut in half the long way:

   4 bananas

4. Arrange the banana halves in the dish.

5. Drizzle over each, using a teaspoon to measure:

   8 teaspoons maple syrup for all

6. Set the timer for 15 minutes, and bake. Serve warm.

☀Banana Pudding

Makes 4 servings

A topping of shredded coconut is the perfect addition to banana pudding.

1. Measure into a bowl:
   - 1/2 **pound tofu, crumbled**
   - 2 **tablespoons canola oil**
   - 2 **tablespoons orange juice**
   - 2 **tablespoons honey**
   - 2 **bananas, sliced**

2. Stir these together, then put half in the blender.

3. Turn the blender on and off to blend. When the blender is off, use a rubber scraper to push the mix down the sides. Blend until the mixture is creamy.

4. Put the pudding into a clean bowl, and blend the rest of the mixture until it is creamy. Then mix the batches together.

☀Graham Cracker Crust

Makes 1 crust

*G*raham cracker crusts are a good choice for pies that have a pudding-like filling.

1. Lightly coat a pie plate with margarine or butter. Heat the oven to 375°.

2. Place in a plastic bag:

   16 square graham crackers, crumbled

   Close the top of the bag, and roll out the crumbs until they are small, using a rolling pin. Put the crumbs in a small bowl.

3. Mix the crumbs with:

   2 tablespoons sugar
   1/3 cup melted margarine or butter

Jodi makes Graham Cracker Crust.

4. With the back of a spoon, press the crumbs evenly into the bottom of the pan and up the sides.

5. Set the timer for 12 minutes, and bake. Remove from the oven and cool before filling.

☀Magic Coconut Pie

Makes 8 servings

This pie makes its own crust and topping as it bakes.

1. Heat the oven to 350°. Oil a pie pan with butter or margarine.

2. Measure into a blender:

   2 cups milk or soymilk

   1/4 cup sugar

   1/4 cup melted butter or margarine

   3 eggs*

   1/2 cup flour

   1 cup unsweetened coconut

   1 teaspoon vanilla

3. Cover the blender, and mix on high speed for 10 seconds. (You can count to 10 slowly.) Pour into the pie pan. Set the timer for 45 minutes, and bake in the hot oven.

*Vegan Alternative: Instead of 3 eggs, use 4 1/2 teaspoons Ener-G Egg Replacer mixed with 1/3 cup water. This will not create the "magic" of an instant crust and topping, but it will still make a delicious coconut cream pie filling. Serve in your favorite regular or graham cracker crust with pineapple sundae topping.

Pumpkin Pie

8 servings

This is best made with a food processor or blender to get a smooth, creamy consistency.

1. Make the pastry crust on page 87, and have it ready in a pie pan.

2. Heat the oven to 400°.

3. Put into a food processor or blender, and process until smooth:

    ³/₄ pound tofu, crumbled

    ¹/₃ cup canola oil

    1 teaspoon salt

4. Blend all at once in the processor, or measure into a bowl and process in 2 batches in a blender:

    1 cup (packed) brown sugar

    3 tablespoons flour

    1 (15-ounce) can pumpkin

    1¹/₂ teaspoons cinnamon

    ³/₄ teaspoon powdered ginger

    ¹/₂ teaspoon nutmeg

    2 teaspoons vanilla extract

5. When the filling is well blended, pour it into the pastry shell. Set the timer for 10 minutes, and bake. Reduce the heat to 350°, reset the timer for 40 to 45 minutes, and continue baking. Serve warm or chilled.

Cheesecake

Makes 8 servings

Who doesn't like cheesecake? This version is made like a pie, so you won't need any of the special pans used to make deli cheesecake.

You will need:

1 Graham Cracker Crust, p. 133

Don't pre-bake it for this cheesecake.

1. Heat the oven to 350°.

2. Mix until smooth and creamy in a food processor, or measure into a bowl and then mix in two batches in a blender:

1 pound tofu, crumbled   **$1/3$ cup honey or sugar**

$1/3$ cup brown sugar, packed   **$1/4$ cup canola oil**

2 tablespoons lemon juice

3. When the mixture is smooth, add:

2 tablespoons flour

1 teaspoon vanilla

$1/4$ teaspoon salt

4. Process until well mixed. If you have made it in two batches, stir them together. Pour it into the crust. Set the timer for 50 minutes, and bake. It's alright if small cracks appear in the top of the filling.

Strawberry Cheesecake

1. Wash and slice:

   2 cups fresh strawberries

   The berries can be sweetened with a little honey or sugar.

2. Arrange on top of the cooled cheesecake.

Chocolate or Carob Chip Cheesecake

1. As soon as the cheesecake comes out of the oven, dot the top with:

   1/2 cup chocolate or carob chips

Melina uses a pastry blender.

Pineapple Upside-Down Cake

Makes 8 servings

1. Heat the oven to 350°.
2. Warm over low heat in a 10-inch ovenproof skillet or in a 9 x 9-inch pan:

   ¹/₄ cup canola oil
3. Sprinkle in evenly:

   ³/₄ cup brown sugar
4. Arrange in the pan over the sugar:

   1 (17-ounce) can pineapple slices, drained
5. Cream together with a big slotted spoon:

   ¹/₂ cup canola oil   **1 cup sugar**
6. Sift onto a piece of waxed paper:

   2 cups flour   **1 tablespoon baking powder**
7. Measure out:

   1 cup milk or soymilk
8. Add half the milk to the creamed mixture, then half the flour, then the rest of the milk and then the rest of the flour, stirring each addition in well. Add:

   1 teaspoon vanilla
9. Pour the batter over the pineapple. Put in the oven. Set the timer for 40 to 45 minutes, and bake. Remove to a board to cool for 5 minutes.
10. Run a knife around the edges of the pan to loosen the cake, then place a large plate over the pan. Using pot holders and with both hands, flip the plate and pan upside down quickly so the cake comes out with the pineapple on top. Cut into 8 wedges or squares, and serve warm.

You can also make this with apricots. Place 9 dried apricot halves inside the pineapple slices in the pan.

☀Lemon Frosting

Makes 2 cups

1. Grate on the smallest holes of grater:
   1 teaspoon (when grated) lemon rind

2. Using a fork, mix it in a small bowl with:
   2 cups powdered sugar   **2 tablespoons lemon juice**
   1 tablespoon water

3. Spread the frosting on the Applesauce Cake, p. 140, with a spatula.

☀Chocolate Frosting

Makes enough to frost a 9 x 13-inch layer cake or two 8-inch layers

1. Heat in a medium-sized pan:
   2 tablespoons butter or margarine
   2 tablespoons milk or soymilk

2. Remove from the heat and beat in a little at a time:
   2 tablespoons cocoa   **2 cups powdered sugar**

3. When the frosting is creamy, stir in:
   1 teaspoon vanilla

4. Drop evenly spaced spoonfuls of the frosting onto the cake, then swirl them together with a spatula.

☀Applesauce Cake

Makes 15 servings

1. Heat oven to 350°. Oil a 9 x 13-inch pan.

2. Cream together with slotted spoon in a big bowl:
    1 stick margarine or butter, softened
    1 cup sugar

3. Sift together onto waxed paper:
    2½ cups flour   **1 teaspoon baking powder**
    1 teaspoon baking soda   **1 teaspoon cinnamon**

4. Add half the flour to the creamed mixture and stir well.

5. Stir in:
    1½ cups applesauce   **¼ cup water**

6. Beat in the rest of the flour. You may add:
    ½ cup raisins   **½ cup chopped walnuts**

7. Spread the batter evenly in the oiled pan.

8. Set the timer for 30 to 35 minutes, and bake until a toothpick stuck in the center comes out clean.

9. Remove to a board and cool, then frost with Lemon Frosting, p.+.

*Vegan Alternative: Instead of 1 egg, you can use ½ tablespoon Ener-G Egg replacer mixed with 2 tablespoons water or 2 teaspoons flaxseed blended with 2 tablespoons warm water until thickened.

Lemon Squares

Makes 9 squares

1. Heat the oven to 350°. Oil an 8 x 8-inch pan.

2. Sift into a 2-quart bowl:

   1 cup flour   **¹/₄ cup powdered sugar**

3. Cream in, using a slotted spoon:

   1 stick margarine or butter, softened

4. When this is well mixed, pat it evenly into the bottom of the baking pan.

5. Set the timer for 20 minutes, and bake this bottom layer.

6. Remove the pan to a board, but don't turn off the oven.

7. While the crust bakes, mix together with a whisk:

   2 beaten eggs*   **1 cup sugar**
   ¹/₂ teaspoon baking powder   **2 tablespoons fresh lemon juice**

   (This filling will be runny.)

8. Pour the mixture into the baked bottom crust.

9. Put the pan back in the oven for 20 minutes (set the timer).

10. Remove from the oven, place on a board, and cool for 30 minutes. If desired, sift over the top:

    1 tablespoon powdered sugar

11. Cut into 9 squares and serve on dessert plates.

*Vegan Alternative: Instead of 2 eggs, you can use 1 tablespoon Ener-G Egg replacer mixed with ¹/₄ cup water or 4 teaspoons flaxseed blended with ¹/₄ cup warm water until thickened.

Strawberry Shortcake

Makes 8 servings

1. Rinse and remove the hulls from:

   1 quart fresh strawberries

2. Cut them in half and sprinkle with:

   2 tablespoons sugar

3. Heat the oven to 400°. Oil an 8-inch layer cake pan well.

4. Sift into a medium-sized bowl:

   2 cups flour   **4 teaspoons baking powder**

   1 teaspoon salt   **2 tablespoons sugar**

5. Cut in with a pastry blender:

   3/4 stick margarine or butter

6. When the mixture is crumbly, stir in:

   3/4 cup milk or soymilk

7. Push the dough into a ball, then flatten it out to a circle to fit the oiled pan.

8. Set the timer for 25 minutes, and bake in the hot oven.

9. Remove from the oven and cool for 5 minutes. Carefully and quickly flip upside down onto a plate, then right side up on the serving plate. Use a long bread knife (the kind with serrated edges) to make 2 layers by slicing through the middle crosswise.

10. Carefully lift off the top half to another plate. Spread the warm bottom layer very gently with:

   Soft margarine or butter

   Spoon half the strawberries over this bottom layer. Gently set the top layer on the berries. Top with the rest of the berries. Serve warm with:

   Ice cream or whipped tofu topping

Cocoa Pudding Cake

Makes 6 servings

This gooey dessert makes its own sauce as it bakes and is a chocolate lover's delight.

1. Heat the oven to 350°. Oil an 8 x 8-inch baking pan.

2. Measure into a bowl and stir well:

    3 tablespoons unsweetened cocoa powder

    1 cup unbleached white flour   3/4 cup sugar

    2 teaspoons baking powder   1/2 teaspoon salt

    2 tablespoons canola oil   1/2 cup milk or soymilk

    1 teaspoon vanilla extract

    Pour this batter into the oiled pan.

3. In a separate bowl, measure and mix:

    3/4 cup firmly packed brown sugar

    1/4 cup unsweetened cocoa powder

4. Sprinkle this sugar mixture over the top of the cake batter.

5. Pour over the sugar mixture:

    1 3/4 cups boiling water

6. Set the timer for 45 minutes. When the cake is done, remove from the oven, and serve warm.

Chocolate Mint Squares

Makes 16 squares

This is a good recipe for learning how to use baking chocolate.

1. Heat the oven to 350°. Oil an 8 x 8-inch pan.

2. Place in a pie pan:

    ¹/₂ cup almonds

    Set the timer for 10 minutes, and roast in the oven. Remove and chop into small pieces. Leave the oven on.

3. Melt in a small pan over low heat:

    1 stick margarine or butter

    2 squares unsweetened baking chocolate

4. Beat with a whisk in a bowl:

    2 eggs

5. Add and beat well:

    1 cup sugar

6. Stir in the melted chocolate. Then add:

    ¹/₂ cup flour

7. Stir in:

    ¹/₂ teaspoon peppermint extract   the chopped almonds

8. Pour into the oiled dish. Set the timer for 25 minutes, and bake. Cool and cut into 16 squares.

Brownies

Makes 16 squares

Making good brownies doesn't have to be difficult

1. Follow directions for Chocolate Mint Squares, on the facing page, but instead of peppermint extract and almonds use:

1 teaspoon vanilla

$1/2$ chopped cup walnuts (Do not roast the walnuts.)

Melina levels the flour for accurate measuring.

Chocolate Bundt Cake

Makes 8 to 12 servings

If you don't have a bundt pan, you can use two 8-inch layer cake pans. Cut out circles of waxed paper to fit in the bottom of each pan, and oil the paper so the cake layers come out easily when cool.

1. Oil a bundt pan carefully. Heat the oven to 350°.

2   In a large bowl, stir together:

    1 1/2 cups sugar   1/2 cup unsweetened cocoa powder
    2 1/2 cups unbleached white flour   1 1/2 teaspoons baking soda
    1/2 teaspoon salt

Make a well in the center.

3. Add to the dry ingredients and stir until the batter is smooth:

    1/2 cup canola oil   1 1/2 cups water
    1 1/2 teaspoons white vinegar   2 teaspoons vanilla extract

4. Pour into oiled bundt pan or 2 prepared 8-inch layer pans.

5. Set the timer for 35 to 40 minutes, and bake. The cake is done when it begins to pull away from the sides of the pan.

6. Cool the cake for 10 minutes. Loosen the sides and center gently with a plastic knife, then invert over a serving plate. If the cake is not allowed to cool, it may break apart coming out of the pan.

Chocolate Chip Cookies

Makes 36 cookies

These are also good with carob chips.

1. Heat the oven to 375°. Lightly oil 2 cookie sheets.

2. Cream with a slotted spoon until well mixed:
    1 stick margarine or butter
    $1/2$ cup sugar
    1 egg*

3. Sift together:
    $1^1/2$ cups flour
    $1^1/2$ teaspoons baking powder
    $1/2$ teaspoon salt

4. Stir the flour into the creamed mixture, and beat well. Add:
    1 tablespoon water
    1 cup chocolate or carob chips
    1 teaspoon vanilla

5. Drop by teaspoonfuls onto the cookie sheets. Set the timer for 10 to 12 minutes, and bake in the hot oven. Don't brown.

*Vegan Alternative: Instead of 1 egg, use $1/2$ tablespoon Ener-G Egg Replacer mixed with 2 tablespoons water or 2 teaspoons flaxseed blended with 2 tablespoons warm water until thickened.

☀Chocolate Chip Bars

Makes 18 bars

Chocolate chips bars are even quicker to make than chocolate chip cookies.

1. Heat the oven to 350°. Oil a 9 x 11-inch pan.

2. Cream together with a slotted spoon in a 2-quart bowl:
   1½ sticks margarine or butter, softened
   ⅔ cup sugar

3. When the mixture is creamy, stir in:
   1 egg*   ¼ cup water

4. Sift together onto a piece of waxed paper:
   2½ cups flour   1½ teaspoons baking powder
   ¼ teaspoon salt

5. Stir flour mixture into the dough until it is well mixed. The dough will be stiff.

6. Stir in:
   1 teaspoon vanilla   8 ounces chocolate or carob chips

7. Spread the dough evenly into the oiled pan.

8. Set the timer for 25 minutes, and bake until golden brown on top.

9. Remove to a board and cool, but cut into 18 bars while still warm.

*Vegan Alternative: Instead of 1 egg, use ½ tablespoon Ener-G Egg Replacer mixed with 2 tablespoons water or 2 teaspoons flaxseed blended with 2 tablespoons warm water until thickened.

☀Firelighters

Makes 18 bars

These got their name because they look like chips of wood for starting a fire, but they are delicious.

1. Heat the oven to 325°. Oil a 9 x 9-inch pan.

2. Combine in a 2-quart bowl with a pastry blender:
   1 stick margarine or butter, softened
   1 tablespoon light corn syrup
   $1/2$ cup brown sugar
   1 teaspoon vanilla

3. Mix together in another bowl:
   $1^3/4$ cups oatmeal
   $1/3$ cup coconut
   $1/2$ teaspoon baking powder

4. Mix the oatmeal mixture and the margarine or butter mixture together.

5. Press the dough into the oiled pan. It will be about a half-inch thick.

6. Set the timer for 20 to 25 minutes, and bake. Don't let them get too brown.

7. Remove the pan to a board, and cool 5 minutes. Cut into 18 bars while warm.

Pecan Rounds

Makes 24 cookies

These make great treats around Christmastime—or any time.

1. Heat the oven to 350°. Lightly oil a cookie sheet.

2. Beat together with a slotted spoon until creamy:
    1 stick margarine or butter, softened
    1 tablespoon honey or brown rice syrup

3. Chop up very small:
    1 cup pecans

4. Add them to the margarine or butter mixture with:
    1 teaspoon vanilla

5. Sift onto waxed paper before measuring:
    1 cup flour

6. Stir the flour into the dough, mixing well. You may use your hands. If the dough is sticky, add a little bit more flour.

7. Shape the dough into 24 small balls. Place the balls on the cookie sheet, and flatten a little.

8. Set the timer for 15 to 20 minutes, and bake but don't brown. Cool the cookies on waxed paper.

Oatmeal Cookies

Makes 70 cookies

1. Heat the oven to 375°. Oil 2 cookie sheets. You will need to use the cookie sheets more than once, but after one batch is removed, wipe off the sheet with a paper towel, then oil it again.

2. Mix together in a large bowl using a slotted spoon:

    2 sticks margarine or butter   **1 packed cup brown sugar**

3. When creamy, add and beat well:

    1 egg*   **1 tablespoon molasses**

    1/4 cup milk or soymilk

4. Measure, add to the bowl, and stir well:

    1 1/2 cups flour   **1/2 teaspoon salt**

    1/2 teaspoon baking soda   **1 teaspoon cinnamon**

    2 cups rolled oats

5. Pour hot water over in a small bowl:

    1 cup raisins

    Drain the raisins well, then stir them in last.

6. Drop the dough by teaspoonfuls onto an oiled cookie sheet, making 20 on one sheet. When one sheet is filled, put it in the preheated oven, and set the timer for 12 minutes. While that batch is baking, you can fill another sheet.

7. Lift the hot cookies carefully with a pancake turner and set them on waxed paper to cool. Put another batch in the oven, and set the timer again.

8. Continue until all the batter is used. Store the cookies in a container with a tight fitting lid.

*Vegan Alternative: Instead of 1 egg, use 1/2 tablespoon Ener-G Egg Replacer mixed with 2 tablespoons water or 2 teaspoons flaxseed blended with 2 tablespoons warm water until thickened.

☀Peanut Butter Cookies

Makes 60 cookies

This makes a lot of cookies, but they're so *yummy*, they won't stay around long.

1. Heat the oven to 375°. Lightly oil 3 cookie sheets.

2. Cream with a pastry blender until well mixed:

   1 stick margarine or butter, softened

   ¹/₂ cup brown sugar   **¹/₂ cup white sugar**

3. Beat into the mixture with a big spoon:

   1 egg*   **1 cup peanut butter**

   1 teaspoon vanilla   **¹/₂ teaspoon salt**

   ¹/₂ teaspoon baking soda

4. Sift onto waxed paper before measuring:

   1¹/₂ cups flour

5. Stir the flour into the dough, then roll the dough into small balls between your hands. Place on the cookie sheets.

6. Gently flatten each ball with a fork, making crisscross marks.

7. Set the timer for 12 to 15 minutes, and bake on the middle rack of the oven. Don't let the cookies get brown. Remove from the pans while warm.

*Vegan Alternative: Instead of 1 egg, use ¹/₂ tablespoon Ener-G Egg Replacer mixed with 2 tablespoons water or 2 teaspoons flaxseed blended with 2 tablespoons warm water until thickened.

Ginger Molasses Cookies

Makes 32 cookies

Be sure to keep these in a tightly closed container so they'll remain soft.

1. Heat the oven to 350°, and set out 2 cookie sheets.

2. Mix together in a large bowl, using a slotted spoon:

   2 cups flour   1 tablespoon powdered ginger
   2 teaspoons baking soda   1 teaspoon cinnamon
   1/2 teaspoon salt   1 cup sugar

3. Measure into the bowl:

   1/2 cup canola oil
   1/4 cup molasses
   1/4 cup water

   Stir well. The dough should be firm and not sticky.

4. Put on a saucer:

   3 tablespoons sugar

5. Wet your hands and shape the dough into 32 little balls. Roll each ball in the sugar, and set it on the unoiled cookie sheets about 2 inches apart.

6. Set the timer for 9 minutes, and bake. Remove the pans from the oven carefully. The cookies will be soft. Let them cool for 2 minutes only, then lift them off the pan onto a plate using a pancake turner.

Gingerbread

Makes 15 servings

If you use the same measuring cup for the molasses and oil and measure the oil first, the molasses will slide right out of the cup.

1. Heat oven to 375°. Oil a 13 x 9 x 2-inch pan.

2. Measure into a large bowl:

    3 cups flour

    2 teaspoons powdered ginger

    1 teaspoon cinnamon

    1 teaspoon salt

2. Stir the dry ingredients together, and add

    ³/₄ cup canola oil

    1 cup molasses

3. Stir together:

    2 teaspoons baking soda

    1¹/₂ cups boiling water

    Stir the hot soda water into the gingerbread mix, about a third at a time, stirring until the mixture is smooth.

4. Pour the batter into the pan, set the timer for 40 to 45 minutes, and bake.

5. Serve with Lemon Sauce, on the facing page, if desired.

Lemon Sauce

Makes about 2$\frac{1}{2}$ cups

Try this traditional topping for Gingerbread, on the facing page, and with the Baked Bananas on p. 131 as well.

1. Mix in a small pan:

    1 cup sugar
    2 tablespoons cornstarch

2. Stir in gradually:

    2 cups water

3. Cook over low heat until the mixture is thick and clear. Remove from the heat.

4. Stir in, blending thoroughly:

    2 tablespoons margarine
    2 tablespoons lemon juice
    2 teaspoons grated lemon peel

Gingerbread Boys & Girls

Makes 24 to 30

If you do not have a cutter, make a pattern by folding stiff paper and drawing half a figure on one side, with its middle on the fold. Make it 5 or 6 inches tall. Cut it out and unfold it, and you will have a symmetrical figure to use as a pattern for cutting.

1. Cream together in a big bowl:

   $1/2$ cup canola oil

   1 cup brown or white sugar

2. Beat in:

   1 cup dark molasses

3. Sift together onto a big piece of waxed paper:

   7 cups flour

   2 teaspoons baking soda

   1 teaspoon cinnamon

   2 teaspoons powdered ginger

   1 teaspoon salt

4. Have ready in a measuring cup:

   $2/3$ cup water

5. Stir $1/3$ of the flour and spice mixture into the bowl, then mix in half of the water. Stir in half of the remaining flour, then the rest of the water. You may have to work in the last of the flour with your hands as the dough will be stiff. Keep the bowl covered with a towel so it doesn't dry out while you are rolling.

6. Heat the oven to 350°. Lightly oil several cookie sheets, and lightly flour a board and rolling pin.

7. Roll out part of the dough about $1/3$-inch thick. Place your pattern on the dough, and with a sharp knife or shaped cutter, cut around it.

8. Using a pancake turner, gently lift the gingerbread figures onto the oiled cookie sheet.

9. Repeat until all the dough is used. Press scraps of dough together to roll out again.

10. When one pan is full, put it in the oven and set the timer for 8 minutes.

11. Remove from the oven. Lift the cookies carefully off the sheet, and cool on waxed paper.

12. When all the cookies have been baked, make:
   Gingerbread Icing, below

13. Decorate the gingerbread kids with a toothpick dipped in icing. Use raisins for eyes if you want.

Gingerbread Icing

1. Stir together in a small bowl, using a fork:
   $1/2$ cup powdered sugar
   1 to 2 teaspoons water
   1 or 2 drops food coloring

Erica and Melina make Popcorn Balls, p 167.

Party Food

Good food makes a good party, and you can share your cooking skills with friends. Fix dips ahead of time, and have a colorful tray of raw vegetables for "dippers." Have crackers and a spread or a plate of fancy sandwiches. Plan on plenty of food for teenage appetites. Make bars or cookies in the dessert section the day before.

☀ indicates easy-to-make recipe

Suggested Party Menu:

Onion Soup Dip, p. 162, with Vegetable "Dippers," p. 162
Crackers with Pink Party Spread, p. 161
Platter of Fancy Sandwiches, below
Oatmeal Cookies, p.151   Brownies, p. 145
Beverages

☀Fancy Sandwiches

1.   Cut crusts from bread. (Save the crusts to make bread crumbs). Use a cookie cutter to make bread rounds. Top with Cucumber Salad slices, p. 111.

2.   Make sandwiches with Tofu Salad, p. 110, and 2 slices of bread, and cut each sandwich on the diagonal to make 4 triangles.

3.   Make Date Nut Bread, p. 26, the day before. The day of the party, slice it thinly and spread with softened cream cheese. Cut each slice into thirds.

4.   Open Face Sandwiches: Cut slices of bread into rounds or triangles, and spread with Olive-Nut spread, p. 161.

5.   Keep sandwiches covered and chilled, so they don't dry out. Just before serving time, decorate the platter with sprigs of parsley.

☀Stuffed Celery

Cut celery stalks into 2-inch lengths. Fill the hollow with Pink Party Spread, below, or peanut butter.

☀Pink Party Spread

Makes about 1 cup

To make onion juice, cut an onion in half and scrape the flat side with a sharp knife over a small bowl.

1. Mash together with a fork:

    1 (8-ounce) package cream cheese or soy cream cheese

    2 tablespoons milk or soymilk

    $1/2$ teaspoon paprika

    $1/2$ teaspoon onion juice

☀Olive Nut Spread

Makes almost 1 cup

1. Combine in a small bowl:

    $1/2$ cup chopped ripe olives or stuffed green olives

    $1/4$ cup chopped walnuts

    2 tablespoons mayonnaise or soy mayonnaise

☀Vegetable Dippers

1. Fix a pretty platter or bowl with your choice of:
   Carrots, peeled and cut in sticks
   Celery, trimmed and cut in sticks
   Green or red pepper, cut in strips
   Cherry tomatoes, whole
   Fresh mushrooms, thickly sliced
   Cucumber, peeled and cut in sticks
   Zucchini, cut in sticks
   Broccoli, broken up into flowers
   Cauliflower, broken up into flowers
   Radishes, with tops trimmed off

☀Onion Soup Dip

Makes 2 cups

1. Stir together until well mixed:
   $1/3$ cup dried onion soup mix
   2 cups sour cream or soy sour cream

2. Cover the bowl and chill 2 hours before serving.

Chile Yogurt Dip

Makes about 2 cups

1. Blend together

    2 cups plain yogurt or soy yogurt

    2 tablespoons olive oil

    2 green onions, chopped

    1 teaspoon chile powder

    1/4 teaspoon black pepper

2. Taste and add a little salt if needed. Chill. Serve with raw veggies.

☀Warm Chili Con Queso Dip

Makes about 2 cups

This is great with corn chips or tortillas.

1. Heat in a small pan:

    1 (8-ounce) jar picante or taco sauce

    1/2 teaspoon garlic powder

2. When it's warm, stir in to melt:

    1 cup (4 ounces) grated Jack cheese or soy Jack cheese

☀Cheese Logs

Makes 6 logs

1. Have ready:

    12 slices thin sliced bread

    12 square slices of cheese or soy cheese

    Mustard

    Margarine or butter, softened

    Toothpicks

2. Heat the oven to 400°.

3. Trim the crusts from the bread. Spread each slice with mustard, and place a slice of cheese on the bread. Pull the 2 opposite corners together, and fasten with a toothpick. Spread the soft margarine or butter on the outside of each log.

4. Place on a baking sheet, set the timer for 10 minutes, and bake until lightly browned.

☀Cheese Dollies

Makes 16

1. Heat the oven to 425°. Oil a baking sheet.

2. Mix with a large spoon:
   1 cup flour
   1 cup grated cheese or soy cheese
   1/2 teaspoon salt
   3/4 cup milk

3. Drop by tablespoons 1 inch apart on the sheet.

4. Set the timer for 7 minutes, and bake until lightly brown. Remove from the baking sheet while warm.

Gretchen mashes cream cheese for Pink Party Spread, p. 161.

☀Mini-Pizzas

Makes 12 servings

This is a quick and easy way to get a pizza treat.

1.   Have ready:

   6 English muffins, cut in half

   1 onion, thinly sliced

   1 green pepper, thinly sliced

   1/2 cup sliced stuffed olives

   1 cup (4 ounces) grated cheese or soy cheese

2.   Mix together in a small bowl:

   1 (8-ounce) can tomato sauce

   1 teaspoon oregano

   1 teaspoon basil

3.   Spread the muffins with the tomato mixture, then arrange the onions, peppers, olives, and cheese on top.

4.   Heat the broiler and place the muffin halves on a cookie sheet. Put under the broiler on an oven rack about 4 inches from the heat, leaving oven door open. Broil until the cheese bubbles. Serve hot.

☀Popcorn Treats

Makes about 1 quart

Use plain unbuttered popcorn to make balls, or try popcorn mixed with raisins and peanuts

1. Heat in a big pot with a secure lid over medium high heat:
   1 tablespoon oil

   Drop in a test kernel to see if the oil is hot enough.

2. When the test kernel pops, pour in:
   ¼ cup popcorn kernels

   Cover the pan and shake until the popping stops.

3. Pour into a big bowl. To serve, melt and stir into the popped corn:
   2 tablespoons margarine or butter

4. Make a double batch to use in Cracker Jack, p. 168.

☀Cracker Jack

Makes 9 cups

1. Mix together in a big bowl:
   2 quarts popped corn
   1 cup roasted peanuts

2. Heat the oven to 350˚.

3. Cook in a small pan a few minutes:
   1 stick melted butter or margarine
   1 teaspoon molasses
   1/3 cup honey or corn syrup

4. Pour the syrup over the popcorn and peanuts, stirring with a big spoon to mix well. Spread the mix out on a cookie sheet. Set the timer for 10 minutes, and bake. It will be crispy when cool.

☀Cheese Corn

1. Sprinkle 4 cups popped corn with:
   2 tablespoons Parmesan cheese or nutritional yeast flakes

Popcorn Balls

Makes 15

1. Pop in two batches using the directions for making popcorn on p. 167:
   $1/2$ cup popcorn kernels

2. Combine in a 1-quart pan:
   2 tablespoons margarine or butter
   $1^{1}/2$ packed cups brown sugar
   6 tablespoons water

3. Stir and cook until it boils. Use caution: The syrup will be very hot. Boil without stirring until it tests for the soft-ball stage. (See step 4.) Test every 2 minutes.

4. To test, have ready:
   1 cup cold water

   Drop a little syrup into the water from a teaspoon, and try to press it into a soft ball. As soon as it will press together, remove the pan from stove.

5. Pour the syrup over the popcorn quickly, mixing with a large spoon, trying to coat every kernel. When it's cool enough to handle, rub a little margarine or butter on your hands, and press the hot corn into balls.

Sesame Seed Crackers

Makes 24 crackers

1. Combine in a bowl using a pastry blender:

   1 stick margarine or butter

   1¹/2 cups flour

   1/2 teaspoon salt

   1 dash cayenne pepper

2. Have ice water in a cup and add only a spoonful or two to the dry ingredients—just enough to moisten it so it forms a ball.

3. Heat the oven to 375°.

4. Lightly oil a cookie sheet. Roll out the dough very thinly between 2 sheets of waxed paper. Cut into squares or diamonds. Lift the pieces carefully onto the baking sheet, and use a fork to prick top of dough all over.

5. Sprinkle evenly over the top:

   2/3 cup sesame seeds

6. Set the timer for 12 to 15 minutes, and bake until lightly browned.

Chocolate Dipped Strawberries

Makes 24

Thﬁs is the most elegant party dish you could serve your guests, and you can make them the day before.

1. Wash, but leave on the green leaves:

    24 large strawberries

    Dry them on paper towels.

2. Melt in a small pan set in a pan of hot water:

    8 ounces chocolate or carob chips

3. Line a platter with waxed paper. Carefully hold each berry by its leaves, and dip it into the melted chocolate, covering the bottom 2/3 of the berry. This leaves some red showing. Place each dipped berry on the waxed paper. Chill before serving.

Stuffed Dates

1. Packaged, pitted dates need not be washed. Stuff each date with large pieces of pecans or walnuts, and press the edges of the dates together. They can be rolled in coconut or powdered sugar, if desired.

2. You can also try filling the dates with peanut butter, shaped by your fingers, or use cream cheese softened with a little orange juice.

Setting the Table

An attractive table sets the stage for the food you have prepared. Follow the diagram to set each place neatly. Use a tablecloth or placemats, and cloth or paper napkins.

Flowers, a house plant, or an arrangement of fresh fruits in a bowl make a pretty centerpiece. Candles add a nice touch. Use protective mats under hot foods, and protect a wooden table with coasters under cold beverages.

INDEX

BOOK PUBLISHING CO.

books that educate, inspire, and empower

To find your favorite books on plant-based cooking and nutrition, raw-foods cuisine, and healthy living, visit:

BookPubCo.com

The New Becoming Vegetarian
Brenda Davis, RD
Vesanto Melina, MS, RD
978-1-57067-144-9 • $21.95

Becoming Vegan
COMPREHENSIVE EDITION
Brenda Davis, RD
Vesanto Melina, MS, RD
978-1-57067-297-2 • $29.95

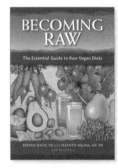

Becoming Raw
Brenda Davis, RD
Vesanto Melina, MS, RD
978-1-57067-238-5 • $24.95

The New Farm Vegetarian Cookbook
Louise Hagler
978-0-913990-60-5 • $12.95

The Tempeh Cookbook
Dorothy Bates
978-0-913990-65-0 • $12.95

Tofu Quick and Easy
REVISED EDITION
Louise Hagler
978-1-57067-112-8 • $12.95

Purchase these titles from your favorite book source or buy them directly from:
Book Publishing Company • PO Box 99 • Summertown, TN 38483 • 1-888-260-8458
Free shipping and handling on all orders